D1744055

Syndicalism In France

Louis Levine

STUDIES IN HISTORY, ECONOMICS AND PUBLIC LAW

EDITED BY THE FACULTY OF POLITICAL SCIENCE
OF COLUMBIA UNIVERSITY

Volume XLVI]   [Number 3

Whole Number 116

SYNDICALISM IN FRANCE

BY

LOUIS LEVINE, Ph.D.

WITH AN INTRODUCTION

BY

PROFESSOR FRANKLIN H. GIDDINGS

SECOND REVISED EDITION

OF

"The Labor Movement in France"

New York

COLUMBIA UNIVERSITY

LONGMANS, GREEN & CO., AGENTS

LONDON: P. S. KING & SON

1914

Copyright, 1912

By

LOUIS LEVINE

PREFACE TO FIRST EDITION

THE term syndicalism sounds strange to an English reader. Its equivalent in English would be Unionism. A syndicat is a union of workingmen, on a trade or on an industrial basis, for the defense of economic interests.

Revolutionary Syndicalism, however, has a broader connotation than the etymology of the term would suggest. A critical analysis of existing institutions, a socialist ideal, and a peculiar conception of revolutionary methods to be used for the realization of the ideal—are all contained in it. Revolutionary Syndicalism appears, therefore, as a phase of the general movement towards a reorganization of society on socialist principles.[1]

Revolutionary Syndicalism cannot be treated, however, exclusively as a phase of the evolution of Socialism. As the term suggests, it is also a devolpment of the French Labor Movement. The organization which represents Revolutionary Syndicalism in France is the General Confederation of Labor (*La Confédération Générale du Travail*, generally referred to as the C. G. T.)—the central organization of the labor unions or syndicats in France. The history of Revolutionary Syndicalism coincides almost entirely with the history of the General Confederation, and it may be said that its future is entirely bound up with the destinies of this organization.

In fact, Revolutionary Syndicalism is an attempt to fuse revolutionary socialism and trade unionism into one co-

---

[1] The term "socialist" is here used in a wide sense to include all varieties, even communistic anarchism.

herent movement. ⟨ Peculiar conditions of French social history have thrown the socialists and anarchists into the syndicats and have secured their leadership there. ⟩ In this respect, Revolutionary Syndicalism is a unique and interesting chapter in the history of both Socialism and Trades unionism and of their mutual relations.

Revolutionary Syndicalism has attracted much attention outside of France. Its more or less rapid development, the turmoil into which it has thrown France several times, the extreme ideas which it expresses, the violent methods it advocates, and its attempts of proselytism outside of France have awakened an interest in it. A number of studies on the movement have appeared in German, Italian, Russian and other European periodicals and books. In English, however, the subject has not received the consideration it would seem to deserve from the theoretical as well as from the practical point of view.

Revolutionary Syndicalism is an aggressive movement. Its aim is to do away with existing institutions and to reconstruct society along new lines. It must, therefore, necessarily call forth a definite attitude on the part of those who become acquainted with it. Those who speak about it are either its friends or its enemies, and even those who want to be impartial towards it are generally unable to resist the flood of sentiment which such a movement sets loose in them.

Impartiality, however, has been the main effort of the writer of this study. It has appeared to him more important to describe the facts as they are and to understand the conditions back of the facts, than to pass sentence whether of approval or of condemnation. He has made the effort, therefore, to suppress his personality entirely in all that part of his work which is purely descriptive. The method adopted has been to describe ideas and facts sympathetically—whether syndicalist or anti-syndicalist, whether promoting or hindering the development of Revolutionary Syndicalism.

The idea that has guided the writer is as follows: Let us imagine that social phenomena could be registered automatically. All social facts would then be recorded with all the sympathies and antipathies with which they are mixed in real life, because the latter are part of the facts. When social descriptions go wrong it is not because they are tinged with feeling, but because they are colored by those feelings which they arouse in the writer and not by those which accompany them in reality. The main task of the writer, therefore, is to try to enter into the feelings which go along with the facts which he is describing.

This means that the writer must alternately feel and think as a different person. However difficult this may be, it is still possible by an effort of imagination prompted by a desire to get at the truth.

This method seems more correct than an attempt to remain entirely indifferent and not to be swayed by any feeling. Indifference does not secure impartiality; it results mostly in colorlessness. For instance, were the writer to remain indifferent or critical while describing the syndicalist ideas, the latter could not be outlined with all the force and color with which they appear in the exposition of their representatives. This would not produce an impartial description, therefore, but a weak and consequently untrue one. On the contrary, by trying to feel and to think as a revolutionary syndicalist, while describing the syndicalist ideas, it is possible to come nearer to reality. The same method is used in the description of anti-syndicalist ideas and efforts.

The result seems to the writer to be the creation of the necessary illusion and the reproduction of the atmosphere in which the movement developed. A critical and personal attitude has been taken only when the writer wished to express his own views. Whether the writer has been more successful than others in this attempt, is for the reader to decide.

From the point of view taken in this essay, Revolutionary Syndicalism has to be described both as a theory and as a practice. The effort is made throughout, however, to consider the theory in close relation to the practice.

The first chapter is introductory and serves merely to give the necessary historical perspective. This explains its brevity.

Revolutionary Syndicalism is undoubtedly a peculiar product of French life and history. Still many of its ideas have a general character and may be of interest to men and women of other countries. After all, the problems that confront the whole civilized world to-day are the same, and the conditions in which their solution has to be tried are everywhere alike in many respects. It has been the writer's sincere hope throughout this work that the history of syndicalism may stimulate the readers of this essay to reflection and criticism that may be of help to them in their efforts to advance the cause of social progress in their own country.

The author wishes to make grateful acknowledgments to Professor Vladimir G. Simkhovitch, Professor Henry Rogers Seager and other professors of Columbia University who have in one way or another aided him in the prosecution of his work; but especially is he indebted to Professor Franklin H. Giddings for invaluable criticisms and suggestions which have guided him throughout his work, and to Professor Edwin R. A. Seligman for encouragement and advice, and help in making it possible for the work to appear in its present form.

NOVEMBER, 1911.   **LOUIS LEVINE.**

PREFACE TO SECOND EDITION

THE term syndicalism no longer needs an introduction to the English reader. Within the past two years it has been naturalized in all English-speaking countries, and has become more or less widely known. It has even been enriched as a result of its migration. In France it simply expressed the comparatively innocent idea of trade unionism, while both in England and America it has come to designate those explosive and aggressive forms of labor unionism which the French described in the words "revolutionary syndicalism." The English use of the term has reacted upon the French syndicalists who have now generally dropped the adjective "revolutionary" and speak of their movement as "le syndicalisme" or "le syndicalisme français." In a word, as a result of recent industrial events the world over, syndicalism has emerged as a new movement of international scope and character. The most significant manifestation of this new development was the first international syndicalist congress which was held in London during the month of September of last year and at which delegates from France, Germany, Holland, Belgium, the United States, England and other countries were present.

The appearance of syndicalist tendencies in other countries has thrown some new light upon the subject. What was considered at one time the peculiar product of France or of the "Latin spirit," appears now to transcend the boundaries of particular countries and of kindred racial groups. It is evidently more closely related to industrial conditions. But its emergence in such countries as England

and the United States destroys the familiar hypothesis that syndicalism is bred only by the small workshop. The latter may explain some peculiar aspects of French syndicalism; it can not explain the methods of direct action and the syndicalist spirit common to all countries.

The explanation seems to me to lie in the direction indicated in the concluding chapter of this book. Three essential causes for the development of French syndicalism are pointed out in it: namely, political disillusionment, the economic weakness of the labor elements, and the comparatively static character of French industry. Recent industrial developments in England and the United States prove that the same conditions explain the appearance of syndicalist tendencies everywhere. The disappointment of the British workers in the political possibilities of the Labor Party, the general mistrust of " politicians " and the actual disfranchisement of large elements of the working population in the United States are facts which are not disputed, and the influence of which in recent industrial events is no longer denied. The comparative weakness of sectional unionism in England and of the unskilled elements in the American labor movement has been brought home to the workers themselves and has determined their change of tactics. Some French syndicalists have criticized the author of this book for laying too much emphasis on the financial weakness of the syndicats in France. But that is a misunderstanding on their part; the emphasis is not on finances, but on weakness which may be the result of many circumstances. Labor unions may have millions in the banks, and still be weak economically on account of the technical conditions of the industry or of the strong organization of the employers. A consciousness of weakness in certain respects must not lead necessarily to submission or to despair. But it generally leads to efforts in new directions and to new methods of action. It has resulted in the amalgamation of unions in England and in the wonderful effort to create a general spirit of solidarity among all elements of labor the world over.

The comparatively static character of industrial life in France has no parallel in England or the United States. This explains why in the latter two countries the ideal aspects of syndicalism have obtained less significance, than in France. In an atmosphere of slow industrial growth, possibilities of immediate industrial gains do not loom up large in the eyes of the workers, and no hope of considerable permanent improvement under given conditions is aroused; on the other hand, the forcible acquisition of the whole industrial equipment and its co-operative management seem comparatively easy.

In the concluding chapter of this book, the possibilities of a change in the character of French syndicalism which were indicated in the first edition are left unchanged. Developments are not yet ripe to warrant any definite conclusion. Of course, some very important phenomena have taken place. The most significant, perhaps, is the development of the iron and steel industry in the eastern parts of France, particularly in the Department Meurthe-et-Moselle. Something very similar to what happened in the steel industry of the United States is happening there; large plants are being erected, gigantic industrial combinations are being formed, labor organizations are relentlessly fought, and foreign workers are imported from Italy, Belgium, Luxembourg, Austria and other countries. Under these conditions, new problems are thrust upon the French labor movement, and it is significant that the Federation of the metal workers has played the leading part in the recent campaign against the " anarchistic " tendencies of the General Confederation of Labor and has demanded·a return to the platform of Amiens (1906) and to a more definite program of labor demands. This does not mean a change in the ideas of French syndicalism, but it certainly indicates a tendency towards the more positive work of organization and of purely trade conquests.

It may be many years, before the struggle of tendencies in the General Confederation of Labor is determined either way. Meanwhile, the significance of French Syndicalism to the world of thought and action has become greater than it was before. France continues to present both the ideas and activities of syndicalism in the most lucid and developed form.

This fact, I take it, has been partly responsible for the keen interest in the first edition of this book and for the necessity of bringing forth a second edition.

LOUIS LEVINE.

NEW YORK CITY, MARCH, 1914.

CONTENTS

CHAPTER I

. THE LABOR MOVEMENT IN FRANCE TO THE COMMUNE (1789–1871)

CHAPTER II

ORIGIN OF THE GENERAL CONFEDERATION OF LABOR (1871–1895)

CHAPTER III

THE FEDERATION OF BOURSES DU TRAVAIL

CHAPTER IV

THE GENERAL CONFEDERATION OF LABOR FROM 1895-1902

CHAPTER V

THE DOCTRINE OF REVOLUTIONARY SYNDICALISM

CHAPTER VI

THE THEORISTS OF REVOLUTIONARY SYNDICALISM

CHAPTER VII

THE GENERAL CONFEDERATION OF LABOR SINCE 1902

CHAPTER VIII

CHARACTER AND CONDITIONS OF REVOLUTIONARY SYNDICALISM

INTRODUCTION

THE democratic social movement has overleaped its platform and escaped out of the hands of its instigators. It is larger than any school of ideas and will not be bound by any program. It can be analyzed in part, and in general terms described, but it can no longer be defined.

Socialism as one phase of this unmanaged and unmanageable tide, has itself been profoundly affected by the magnitude, the complexity, and the waywardness of the mass motion. It now has its "Right" and its "Left." There is a conservative, and there is a radical socialism. Each proclaims the class struggle, and both demand the collective ownership of the chief means of production. But conservative socialism lays stress upon collective ownership, and would move toward it by peaceful, evolutionary steps. It relies on the ballot, believes in legislation, in law, and in government; while radical socialism proclaims "the revolution," plans for the general strike, and preaches the expediency of sabotage and violence.

At first sight almost identical with radical socialism is Syndicalism, which, however, proves upon examination to be both more and less than any socialistic program. In its most characteristic expression, syndicalism denies the state and would substitute for it a purely voluntary collectivism. So far it is at one with anarchism, and there are those who conceive of syndicalism as an anarchistic movement in opposition to socialism. The trade-union organization of labor the world over is looked upon by the syndicalist as the natural basis and agency of his enterprise, quite as existing political organizations are accepted by the conservative or parliamentary socialist as the best preliminary norms from which to evolve a new social order.

In this division of the forces of social democracy into right and left groups over the question of organization and control, we have a significant demonstration of the inadequacy of that Marxian analysis which resolves all social conflict into the antagonism of economic classes. More profound than that antagonism, and in the order of time more ancient, is the unending warfare between those who believe in law and government for all, and those who believe in law and government for none. The more or less paradoxical character of the socialistic movement at the present moment is attributable to the circumstance that, for the time being, these antagonistic forces of socialism and anarchism are confronting a common enemy—the individualist, who believes in law and government for everybody but himself.

To describe, explain and estimate a phenomenon so complex as modern revolutionary syndicalism is a task from which the economist and the historian alike might well shrink. To understand it and to enable readers to understand it is an achievement. I think that I am not speaking in terms of exaggeration in saying that Dr. Levine has been more successful in this arduous undertaking than any predecessor. His pages tell us in a clear and dispassionate way what revolutionary syndicalism is, how it began, and how it has grown, what its informing ideas and purposes are, and by what methods it is forcing itself upon the serious attention of the civilized world. I think that it is a book which no student of affairs can afford to overlook, or to read in any other spirit than that of a sincere desire to know what account of the most profound social disturbance of our time is offered by a competent reporter of the facts.

FRANKLIN H. GIDDINGS.

COLUMBIA UNIVERSITY.

CHAPTER I

THE LABOR MOVEMENT IN FRANCE TO THE COMMUNE
(1789-1871)

THE economic legislation of the French Revolution was guided by individualistic ideas which expressed the interests of the rising middle classes who felt a necessity of removing the obstacles in the way of economic initiative and of personal effort. These interests and ideas dictated the law of March 2-17, 1791, which abolished the guilds and inaugurated the era of competition in France (*Liberté du Travail*). The law declared that henceforth everybody was "free to do such business, exercise such profession, art, or trade, as he may choose."[1]

The abolition of the guilds cleared the way for the technical changes that had just begun and the development of which was yet in the future. These changes may be summarized as the application of science to industry and the introduction of machinery. The process went on in France irregularly, affecting different industries and different localities in various degrees. The first machine (*machine à vapeur*) was introduced in France about 1815; in 1830 there were about 600 in operation. Some idea of the later changes may be gained from the following table giving the number of machines in France from 1839 to 1907:

[1] *Les Associations Professionelles Ouvrières*, Office du Travail (Paris, 1899), vol. i, p. 7.

Year	No. of Machines	Total Horsepower
1839	2,450	33,000
1851	5,672	71,000
1861	15,805	191,000
1871	26,146	316,000
1881	44,010	576,000
1891	55,967	916,000
1901	75,866	1,907,000
1910	82,238	2,913,013 [1]

The introduction of machinery meant the absorption of a larger part of the population in industry, the concentration of industry in a smaller number of establishments and the absolute and relative increase in the numbers of the working population of France.

This class of the population was regulated in its economic action for nearly a century by another law passed June 14-17, 1791, and known by the name of its author as the law Le Chapelier. The law Le Chapelier, though dictated by the same general interests and ideas as the law on the guilds, was made necessary by special circumstances.

The abolition of the guilds had as one of its effects an agitation among the journeymen for higher wages and for better conditions of employment. During the summer of 1791, Paris was the scene of large meetings of journeymen, at which matters of work and wages were discussed. The movement spread from trade to trade, but the struggle was particularly acute in the building trades. Profiting by the law of August 21, 1790, which gave all citizens the " right to assemble peacefully and to form among themselves free associations subject only to the laws which all citizens must obey," [2] the carpenters formed *L'Union fraternelle des ouvriers en l'art de la charpente*, an associa-

---

[1] *Annuaire Statistique.*

[2] *Les Associations Professionelles*, vol. i, p. 8.

tion ostensibly for benevolent purposes only, but which in reality helped the carpenters in their struggle with their masters. The masters repeatedly petitioned the municipality of Paris to put an end to the " disorders," and to the " tyranny " of the journeymen. The masters complained that a general coalition of 80,000 workingmen had been formed in the capital and that the agitation was spreading to the provincial towns.[1] The municipal authorities tried to meet the situation, but their " notices " and " decrees " had no effect. They then appealed to the Constituent Assembly for a general law on associations and combinations. The result was the law Le Chapelier.

The report by which the bill was introduced brought out very clearly the individualistic ideas by which the legislators of the Revolution were inspired. "Citizens of certain trades," read this report, " must not be permitted to assemble for their pretended common interests. There is no longer any corporation (guild) in the State; there is but the particular interest of each individual and the general interest. . . ." And further, " It is necessary to abide by the principle that only by free contracts, between individual and individual, may the workday for each workingman be fixed; it is then for the workingman to maintain the agreement which he had made with his employer."[2]

The law identified the new combinations with the ancient guilds. Its first clause declared that "whereas the abolition of all kinds of corporations of citizens of the same estate (*état*) and of the same trade is one of the fundamental bases of the French Constitution, it is prohibited to reestablish them *de facto* under any pretext or form whatsoever ". The second clause formulated the prohibition to

[1] H. Lagardelle, *L'Évolution des Syndicats Ouvriers en France* (Paris, 1901), p. 13.

[2] *Les Associations Professionelles*, vol. i, pp. 11-12.

form trade organizations in terms which left nothing to be desired in clearness and precision. It read: " The citizens of the same estate or trade, entrepreneurs, those who run a shop, workingmen in any trade whatsoever, shall not, when assembled together, nominate presidents, nor secretaries, nor syndics, shall not keep any records, shall not deliberate nor pass resolutions nor form any regulations with reference to their pretended common interests." The fourth clause declared all acts contrary to this law unconstitutional, subject to the jurisdiction of the police tribunals, punishable by a fine of 500 *livres* and by a temporary suspension of active rights of citizenship. The sixth and seventh clauses determined higher penalties in cases of menace and of violence. The eighth clause prohibited all " gatherings composed of artisans, of workingmen, of journeymen or of laborers, or instigated by them and directed against the free exercise of industry and work to which all sorts of persons have a right under all sorts of conditions agreed upon by private contract (*de gré a gré*) ". " Such gatherings are declared riotous, are to be dispersed by force, and are to be punished with all the severity which the law permits." [1]

After the law was passed by the Assembly, the author of the law, Le Chapelier, added:

I have heard some say that it would be necessary to make an exception in favor of the Chambers of Commerce in cities. Certainly you understand well that none of us intend to prevent the merchants from discussing their common interests. I therefore propose to insert into the proceedings the following clause: " The National Assembly, considering that the law which it has just passed does not concern the Chambers of Commerce, passes to the order of the day."

---

[1] *Les Associations Professionelles*, vol. i, pp. 13-14.

The proposition was adopted. " This last vote," remarks the official historian of the *Office du Travail*, " demonstrates sufficiently that the law was especially directed against the meetings, associations and coalitions of workingmen." [1]

The determination to prevent collective action on the part of the workingmen also guided the legislative activity of Napoleon. In 1803, during the Consulate, a law was passed against coalitions; the same law contained a provision whereby all workingmen were to have a special certificate (*livret*) [2] which subjected them to a strict surveillance of the police. The law of 1803 against coalitions was replaced in 1810 by the clauses 414-416 of the Penal Code which prohibited and punished all kinds of coalitions. These articles which made strikes and all collective action a crime, and which showed clearly discrimination against workingmen, were as follows:

Art. 414. Any coalition among those who employ workingmen, tending to force down wages unjustly and abusively, followed by an attempt or a commencement of execution, shall be punished by imprisonment from six days to one month and by a fine of 200 to 3,000 francs.

Art. 415. Any coalition on the part of the workingmen to cease work at the same time, to forbid work in a shop, to prevent the coming or leaving before or after certain hours and, in general, to suspend, hinder or make dear labor, if there has been an attempt or a beginning of execution, shall be punished by imprisonment of one month to three months maximum; the leaders and promoters shall be punished by imprisonment of two to five years, and

Art. 416. There shall also be subject to penalty indicated in the preceding article and according to the same distinctions,

[1] *Les Associations Professionelles*, vol. i, p. 14.

[2] The obligation of the *livret* was abolished in 1890. G. Weill, *Histoire du Movement Social en France* (Paris, 1904), p. 332.

those workingmen who shall have declared fines, prohibitions, interdictions and any other proscriptions under the name of condemnations and under any qualification whatsoever against the directors of the shops and employers, or against each other.

In the case of this article as well as in that of the preceding, the leaders and promoters of the crime, after the expiration of their fine, may be made subject to the surveillance of the police for two years at least and five years at most.[1]

The prohibition against combination and organization was aggravated for the workingmen by articles 291-294 of the Penal Code which forbade any kind of associations of more than twenty persons. These articles were made more stringent by the Law of 1834 which prohibited associations even of twenty persons, if they were branches of a larger association.[2]

The workingmen, however, soon began to feel that the *Liberté dú Travail* as interpreted by the laws of the country put them at a disadvantage in the struggle for existence. Individually each one of them was too weak to obtain the best bargain from his employer. This was notoriously so in the industries in which machinery was making headway, but the relations between employer and workingmen were aggravated by competition even in those industries where the old conditions of trade did not change perceptibly for some time. Competition forced the employer to become a " calculator above everything else " and " to consider the workingman only from the point of view of the real value which his hands had on the market without heed to his human needs." [3] The workingman, on the other

---

[1] *Les Associations Professionelles*, vol. i, pp. 18-19.

[2] *Ibid.*, pp. 19-20, and p. 26.

[3] M. Du Cellier, *Histoire des Classes Laborieuses en France* (Paris, 1860), p. 362.

custom of traveling which became prevalent among the journeymen of France about that time.[1]   A journeyman (called *compagnon* in French) would usually spend some time in visiting the principal cities of France (make his *tour de France*) to perfect himself in his trade.   A traveling *compagnon* would be in need of assistance in many cases and the *compagnonnages* owed their development to the necessity of meeting this want.

The *compagnonnages* consisted of bachelor journeymen only.   If a member married or established himself as master, he left the *compagnonnage*.   Besides, admission to the *compagnonnage* was dependent on tests of moral character and of technical skill.   Thus, the *compagnonnages* always embraced but a small part of the workingmen—the élite from the technical point of view.   To attain the required technical standard, members had to pass some time as aspirants before they could become *compagnons*.

The organization of the *compagnonnages* was very simple.   All the *compagnons* of the same trade lived together in one house, usually in an inn, kept by the so-called *mère* (mother) or *père* (father) of the trade.   The *compagnons* were generally the only boarders in the house.   If not numerous enough to occupy the entire house, they had one hall for their exclusive occupation.   Here they held their meetings, initiated new members, and kept their records and treasury.   Here, also, *compagnons* arriving from other towns made themselves " recognized " by special signs and symbols.

All the *compagnons* of France were divided among three " orders " called *devoirs*.   The *devoirs* had strange names indicating the legends with which the origins of

[1] Octave Festy, *Le Movement Ouvrier au Début de la Monarchie de France* (Paris, 1900), vol. i, pp. 600 *et seq.*

these organizations were connected. The *devoir*, "Sons of Master Jack " (*Enfants de Maître Jacques*) was founded, according to the story, by one of the master-builders of King Solomon's Temple. The " Sons of Solomon " (*Enfants de Solomon*) were sure that their order was founded by King Solomon himself. The "Sons of Master Soubise" regarded another builder of Solomon's Temple as the founder of their *devoir*. Each *devoir* consisted of a number of trades, and sometimes one and the same trade was divided between two *devoirs*.

Ceremonies and rites constituted an inseparable part of the *compagnonnages*. The initiation of a new member, the " recognition " of a newly arrived *compagnon*, the meeting of two traveling *compagnons* on the road, etc., were occasions for strange and complicated ceremonies which had to be accurately performed. These ceremonies were due in a large measure to the secrecy in which the *compagnonnages* developed under the ancient régime, persecuted as they were by the royal authorities, by the church, and by the master-craftsmen.

Within the *compagnonnages* the feeling of corporate exclusiveness and the idea of hierarchical distinctions were strong. Emblems of distinction, such as ribbons, canes, etc., were worn on solemn occasions, and the way in which they were worn, or their number, or color, indicated the place of the *compagnonnage* within the whole corporate body. Many riots and bloody encounters were occasioned between *devoir* and *devoir* and between different *compagnonnages* within each *devoir* by disputes over " ribbons " and other emblems appropriate to each. For instance, the joiners were friends of the carpenters and of the stonecutters, but were enemies of the smiths whom the other two trades accepted. The smiths rejected the harness-makers. The blacksmiths accepted the wheelwrights on condition that the latter wear their colors in a low buttonhole; the wheelwrights promised but did not keep their promise; they wore their colors as high as the blacksmiths; hence hatred and quarrels. The carpenters wore their colors in their hats; the winnowers wanted to wear them in the same way; that was enough to make them sworn enemies.[1] Besides, the *compagnonnages* did not strive to embrace all members of the same trade or all trades. On the contrary, they were averse to initiating a new trade and it sometimes took decades before a new trade was fully admitted into the organization.

While these features harked back to the past, the economic functions of the *compagnonnages* anticipated and really were a primitive form of the later syndicat. The *compagnonnages* offered effective protection to the *compagnons* in hard stresses of life as well as in their difficulties with their masters. " The ' devoir ' of the compagnons " (read the statutes of one of these societies) " is a fraternal alliance which unites us all by the sacred ties of friendship, the foundations of which are: virtue, frankness, honesty, love of labor, courage, assistance and fidelity." [2] These abstract terms translated themselves in life into concrete deeds of mutual aid and of assistance which were immensely valuable to the traveling *compagnons*. A traveling *compagnon,* on arriving at a city or town, would only have to make himself " recognized " and his fellow-compagnons would take care of him. He would be given lodging and food. Employment would be found for him. If sick or in distress, he would receive aid. If he wished to leave the town to continue his *tour de France,* he would be assisted and would be accompanied some distance on the road.

[1] *Les Associations Professionelles,* vol. i, p. 95.

[2] Maxime Leroy, *Syndicats et Services Publics* (Paris, 1909), p. 12.

With their simple organization, the *compagnons* were able to exert a strong economic influence. They served as bureaus of employment. One *compagnon,* elected *rouleur,* was charged with the duty of finding employment for *compagnons* and " aspirants ". He kept a list of those in need of work and placed them in the order of their inscription. Usually the masters themselves addressed the *rouleurs* for workingmen, when in need of any.

This fact gave the *compagnonnages* a control over the supply of labor. They could withhold labor from a master who did not comply with their demands. They could direct their members into other towns of the *Tour* if necessary, as everywhere the *compagnons* would find friends and protection. They could, therefore, organize strikes and boycott a master or workshop for long periods of time. In fact, by these methods the *compagnonnages* struggled for higher wages and better conditions of employment as far back as the sixteenth century. During the Great Revolution the *compagnonnages* existed in twenty-seven trades and directed the strike-movement described above. They attained the height of their development during the first quarter of the nineteenth century when they were the only effective workingmen's organizations exerting an influence in the economic struggles of the time.

The *compagnonnages* persisted in several trades during the larger part of the nineteenth century. After 1830, however, their influence declined. The new industrial conditions reduced the significance of the personal skill of the workingmen, shifted the boundaries of the ancient trades, and entirely transformed most of them. The rapid development of the modern means of communication made the *tour de France* in its old form an anachronism. The spread of democratic and secular ideas brought the medieval usages and ideas of the *compagnonnages* into disrepute and ridi-

cule. Several attempts to reform the *compagnonnages* and
to bring them into harmony with the new conditions of life
were made by members of the organization, but with no
results.[1]

While the *compagnonnages* were reconstituting themselves during the Consulate and the First Empire, another
form of organization began to develop among the workingmen. This was the friendly or benevolent society for
mutual aid especially in cases of sickness, accident or death.
Several such societies had existed before the Revolution
and the law Le Chapelier was directed also against them.
" It is the business of the nation," was the opinion of Le
Chapelier, accepted by the Constituent Assembly, " it is the
business of the public officials in the name of the nation to
furnish employment to those in need of it and assistance to
the infirm ".[2] Friendly societies, however, continued to
form themselves during the nineteenth century. They
were formed generally along trade lines, embracing members of the same trade. In a general way the government
did not hinder their development.

Mrs. Beatrice Webb and Mr. Sidney Webb have shown
that a friendly society has often been the nucleus of a trade
union in England. In France the friendly societies for a
long time played the part of trade unions. The charge of
promoting strikes and of interfering with industrial matters
was often brought against them.[3] There were 132 such
trade organizations in Paris in 1823 with 11,000 members,
and their numbers increased during the following years.

The form of organization called into being by the new

---

[1] On the *compagnonnage* see, J. Connay, *Le Compagnonnage*, 1909;
E. Martin St. Leon, *Le Compagnonnage*, 1901; Agricol Perdigiuer, *Le
Livre du Compagnonnage*, 1841.

[2] *Les Assoc. Profess.*, vol. i, p. 193.   [3] *Ibid.*, p. 199.

,economic conditions was the *société de resistance,* an organization primarily designed for the purpose of exercising
control over conditions of employment. These societies of
resistance assumed various names. They usually had no
benefit features or passed them over lightly in their statutes.
They emphasized the purpose of obtaining collective con-
'tracts, scales of wages, and general improvements in conditions of employment. These societies were all secret, but
free from the religious and ceremonial characteristics of the
compagnonnages.

One of the most famous of these societies in the history
of the French working-class was the *Devoir Mutuel,*
founded by the weavers of Lyons, in 1823. This society
directed the famous strikes of the weavers in 1831 and
1834. Its aim, as formulated in its statutes, was: first, to
practice the principles of equity; second, to unite the weavers' efforts in order to obtain a reasonable wage for their
labor; third, to do away with the abuses of the factory, and
to bring about other improvements in "the moral and phy-
sical condition " of its members. The society had 3,000
members in 1833.[1]

In 1833 the smelters of copper in Paris formed themselves into a society which was to help them in their resistance against employers. Two francs a day was to be
paid to every member who lost employment because he
did not consent to an unjust reduction in his wages or for
any other reason which might be regarded as having in
view the support of the trade; in other cases of unemployment, no benefit was allowed, in view of the fact that in
ordinary times the smelters were seldom idle.[2] The society
was open to all smelters, without any limitation of age; it

---

[1] *Les Associations Professionelles,* vol. i, pp. 201-203.

[2] *Ibid.,* vol. i, p. 204.

was administered by a council assisted by a commission of representatives from the shops, elected by the members of the society of each shop. The society was soon deprived, however, of its combative character by the government.[1]

A strong society of resistance was organized by the printers of Paris in 1839. Though secret, it gained the adherence of a large part of the trade. In 1848 it had 1,200 members—half of all the printers at that time in Paris. It was administered by a committee. Through its initiative a mixed commission of employers and workingmen was organized which adopted a general scale of wages. This commission also acted as a board of mediation and conciliation in disputes between employers and workingmen.[2]

The *compagnonnages, mutualités* and resistance-societies aimed partly or exclusively to better conditions of employment by exerting pressure upon employers. These societies reveal the efforts that were being made by workingmen to adjust themselves to the economic conditions of the time. But after 1830, other ideas began to find adherents among the French workingmen; namely, the ideas of opposition to the entire economic régime based on private property and the idea of substituting for this system a new industrial organization.

The history of the socialist movement of France before 1848 can not here be entered into. It has been written and rewritten and is more or less known. For the purposes of this study, it is only necessary to point out that during this period, and particularly during the revolutionary period of 1848, the idea of co-operation, as a means of

---

[1] *Les Associations Professionelles*, vol. i, p. 204.

[2] *Ibid.*, pp. 205-6.

abolishing the wage system, made a deep impression upon the minds of French workingmen.[1]

The idea of co-operation had been propagated before 1848 by the Saint-Simonists and Fourierists, and particularly by Buchez who had outlined a clear plan of co-operation in his paper *L'Européen* in 1831-2. Similar ideas were advanced during the forties by a group of workingmen who published *L'Atelier*. But only with the outbreak of the Revolution of 1848, and under the influence of Louis Blanc, did the co-operative idea really become popular with the workingmen. Between 1848 and 1850 the enthusiasm for co-operative societies was great, and a considerable number of them were formed. On July 6, 1848, the Constituent Assembly voted a loan of 3,000,000 francs for co-operative societies, and this sum was divided among 26 societies in Paris and 36 in the provinces.[2] But the number of those founded without assistance was much greater; about 300 in Paris and many more in the provinces. Of these societies most perished within a short time while the rest were dissolved by the administration of Napoleon III after the *coup-d'état* of 1851.[3]

The Revolution of 1848 was an important moment in the history of the French working-class. Though the socialist idea of the " Organization of Work " (*L'Organisation du Travail*) which was so prominent during the Revolution passed into history after the days of June, it left an impression upon the minds of French workingmen. The belief in a possible social transformation became a tra-

---

[1] On the history of French socialism: R. T. Ely, *French and German Socialism* (1878); Th. Kirkup, *A History of Socialism* (1906); G. Isambert, *Les Idées Socialistes en France* (1905); P. Louis, *Histoire du Socialisme Français* (1901).

[2] Georges Renard, *La République de 1848*.

[3] Albert Thomas, *Le Second Empire* (Paris, 1907).

dition with them.   Besides, the Revolution gave a strong impulse to purely trade organizations such as the *sociétés de résistance*.   Before 1848 they had existed in a few trades only.   The period of the Revolution witnessed the formation of a large number of them in various trades and strengthened the tendency towards organization which had manifested itself before.

During the first decade of the Second Empire all workingmen's organizations were prosecuted; most of them perished; others went again into secrecy or disguised themselves as mutual aid societies.

With the advent of the second decade of the Empire the labor movement acquired an amplitude it had never had before.   Its main characteristic during this period was a decided effort to break the legal barriers in its way and to come out into the open.   The workingmen's chief demands were the abolition of the law on coalitions and the right to organize.

The workingmen were given an opportunity to express their views and sentiments on occasions of National and International Exhibitions.   It had become a custom in France to send delegations of workingmen to such exhibitions.   In 1849 the Chamber of Commerce of Lyons sent a delegation of workingmen to the National Exhibition in Paris.   In 1851 the municipality of Paris sent some workingmen to the International Exhibition in London.   A delegation was sent again to London in 1862 and to Paris in 1867.

The workingmen-delegates published reports in which they formulated their views on the condition of their respective trades and expressed their demands and aspirations.   These reports have been called the *cahiers* of the working-class.   The authors of the reports—workingmen themselves, elected by large numbers of workingmen—were representatives in the true sense of the term and voiced the sentiments and ideas of a large part of the French workingmen of their time.

The reports published by the delegates of 1862 contain a persistent demand for freedom to combine and to organize. The refrain of all the reports is: " Isolation kills us ".[1] The trade unions of England made a deep impression on the French delegates and strengthened their conviction of the necessity of organization. " Of 53 reports emanating from 183 delegates of Paris, 38 by 145 delegates express the desire that syndical chambers be organized in their trades." [1]

The government of the Empire, which hoped to interest the workingmen in its existence, gave way before their persistent demands.   In 1864, in consequence of a strike of Parisian printers which attracted much public attention, the old law on coalitions was abolished and the right to strike granted.

The right to strike, however, was bound up with certain other rights which the French workingmen were still denied.   Unless the latter had the right to assemble and to organize, they could profit but little by the new law on coalitions.   Besides, the French workingmen were generally averse to strikes.   The reports of 1862, though demanding the freedom of coalition, declared that it was not the intention of the workingmen to make strikes their habitual procedure.   The delegates of 1867, who formed a commission which met in Paris for two years, discussing all the economic problems that interested the workingmen of the time, were of the same opinion.   A special session of the Commission was devoted to the consideration of the means by which strikes might be avoided.   All agreed that, as one

[1] G. Weill, *op. cit.*, pp. 63-65.

of the delegates expressed it, strikes were "the misery of the
workingmen and the ruin of the employer "[1] and should
be resorted to only in cases of absolute necessity.   What
the delegates demanded was the right to organize and to
form " syndical chambers ".   They hoped that with the
help of these organizations, they would avoid strikes and
improve their economic condition.

In the beginning of 1868, a number of delegates to the
Exhibition of 1867 were received by the Minister of Agriculture, Commerce and Public Works to present their
views and demands.   The vice-president of the Commission, M. Parent, indicated clearly what the workingmen
meant by " syndical chambers " in the following words:

We all agree to proceed by way of conciliation, but we all have
also recognized the necessity of guaranteeing our rights by a
serious organization which should give the workingmen the
possibility of entering easily and without fear into agreement
with the employers. . . . It is thus in order to avoid strikes,
guaranteeing at the same time the wages of the workingmen,
that the delegates of 1867 solicit the authorization to establish
syndicats in each trade in order to counter-balance the formidable organization of the syndical chambers of the merchants and manufacturers. . . . The workingmen's syndical
chambers, composed of syndics elected by the votes of the
workingmen of their trade, would have an important rôle to
fulfil.   Besides the competent experts which they could always
furnish for the cases subject to the jurisdiction of the
prud'hommes, for justices of the peace and for the tribunals
of Commerce, they could furnish arbiters for those conflicts
which have not for their cause an increase in wages.   Such
are: the regulations of the workshops, the use of health-en-
dangering materials, the bad conditions of the machinery and

[1] *Commission Ouvrière de 1867, Recueil des Procès-Verbaux,* vol.
i, p. 28.

of the factory which affect the health of the workingmen and often endanger their lives, the protection of the inventions made by workingmen, the organization of mutual and professional education, which cannot be entirely instituted without the help of the men of the workshop, etc.[1]

On the 30th of March, 1868, the Minister of Commerce and Public Works announced that without modifying the law on coalitions, the government would henceforth tolerate workingmen's organizations on the same grounds on which it had heretofore tolerated the organizations of employers. With this act began the period of toleration which lasted down to 1884, when the workingmen's organizations were brought under the protection of a special law.

The declaration of toleration gave free scope to the workingmen to form their syndical chambers. Some syndicats had been openly formed before. In 1867, the shoemakers had formed a society—the first to bear the name of syndicat—which had openly declared that it would support members on strike and would try to defend and to raise wages. But only after the declaration of the government in 1868 did these societies begin to increase in numbers.

While organizing for resistance, the workingmen during this period, however, placed their main hopes in co-operation; the co-operative society of production was to them the only means of solving the labor question. As one of the delegates to the Workingmen's Commission of 1867 put it: " Salvation is in association " (*Le salut c'est l'association*).[2] The main function of the syndical chamber was to promote the organization of co-operative societies.

The revival of enthusiasm for co-operative societies began

---

[1] Lagardelle, *Évolution des Syndicats*, pp. 218-9.
[2] *Commission Ouvrière de 1867*, vol. i, p. 28.

in 1863. Men of different political and economic views helped the movement. It found supporters in liberal economists, like M. Say and M. Walras; it was seconded by Proudhon and his followers, while a number of communists took an active part in it. Profiting by the experience of 1848-50, the workingmen now adopted a new plan. The co-operative society of production was to be the crowning part of the work, resting upon a foundation of several other organizations. First the members of one and the same trade were to form a syndical chamber of their trade. The syndical chamber was to encourage the creation of a " society of credit and savings " which should have for its aim the collection of funds by regular dues paid by the members. Such " societies of credit and savings " began to develop after 1860, and they were considered very important; not only because they provided the funds, but also and mainly because they helped the members to become acquainted with one another and to eliminate the inefficient. With a society of credit in existence, it was deemed necessary to create a co-operative of consumption. The productive co-operative society was to complete this series of organizations which, supporting one another, were to give stability to the entire structure.

The plan was seldom carried out in full. Co-operatives of production were formed without any such elaborate preparation as outlined above. However, many " societies of credit and saving " were formed. In 1863 there were 200 of them in Paris; and in September, 1863, a central bank, *La Société du Credit au Travail* was organized. Similar central banks were formed in Lyons, Marseilles, Lille and other large cities.

In Paris the *Credit au Travail* became the center of the co-operative movement between 1863 and 1868. It subsidized successively *L'Association* (Nov., 1864-July, 1866)

and *La Co-opération* (Sept., 1866-Feb., 1867)—magazines
devoted to the spread of co-operative ideas.   It gave advice
and information for forming co-operatives.   Most of the
co-operative enterprises of the period were planned and
first elaborated in the councils of this society.   Finally it
furnished the co-operatives with credit.   Its business done
in 1866 amounted to 10½ million francs.[1]

In 1868 the co-operative movement, after several years
of development, suffered a terrible blow.   On November
2nd, the *Credit au Travail* became bankrupt; it had im-
mobilized its capital, and had given out loans for too long
periods, while some of the other loans were not reim-
bursed.   The bank had to suspend payment and was closed.
The disaster for the co-operative movement was complete.
The *Credit au Travail* seemed to incarnate the co-operative
movement; " and its failure made many think that the co-
operative institution had no future ".[2]

The failure of the co-operative movement turned the
efforts of the workingmen into other channels.   They now
began to join the " International Association of Workingmen " in increased numbers and to change their ideas and
methods.

The " International ", as is well known, was formed in
1864 by French and English workingmen.   The French
section, during the first years of its existence, was composed mainly of the followers of Proudhon, known as *mutuellistes*.   The program of the *mutuellistes* was a peaceful
change in social relations by which the idea of justice—conceived as reciprocity or mutuality of services—would be
realized.   The means advocated were education and the
organization of mutual aid societies, of mutual insurance

---

[1] P. Hubert-Valleroux, *La Cöopération* (Paris, 1904), pp. 14-17.

[2] P. Hubert-Valleroux, *op. cit.*, p. 16.

companies, of syndicats, of co-operative societies and the like. Much importance was attached to the organization of mutual credit societies and of popular banks. It was hoped that with the help of cheap credit the means of production would be put at the disposal of all and that co-operative societies of production could then be organized in large numbers. The *Mutuellistes* emphasized the idea that the social emancipation of the workingmen must be the work of the workingmen themselves. They were opposed to state intervention. Their ideal was a decentralized economic society based upon a new principle of right—the principle of mutuality—which was "the idea of the working-class ".[1] Their spokesman and master was Proudhon who formulated the ideas of *mutuellisme* in his work, *De la Capacité Politique des Classes Ouvrières.*

Between 1864 and 1868, the "International" met with little success in France. The largest number of adherents obtained by it during this period was from five to eight hundred. Persecuted by the government after 1867, it was practically dead in France in 1868.[2] But in 1869 it reappeared with renewed strength under the leadership of men of collectivist and communist ideas, which were partly a revival and survival of the ideas of 1848, partly a new development in socialist thought.

One current of communist ideas was represented by the Blanquists. Blanqui, a life-long conspirator and an ardent republican who had been the leader of the secret revolutionary societies under the Monarchy of July, took up his revolutionary activity again during the latter part of the Second Empire. A republican and revolutionary above everything else, he had, however, gradually come to for-

---

[1] P. J. Proudhon, *De la Capacité Politique des Classes Ouvrières* (Paris, 1865), p. 59.

[2] A. Thomas, *Le Second Empire*, p. 332.

mulate in a more precise way a communistic program, to be realized by his party when by a revolutionary upheaval it would be carried into power. The Blanquists denounced the " co-operators " and the " mutuellistes " and called upon the workingmen to organize into secret societies ready, at a favorable moment, to seize political power. Towards the end of the Second Empire, the Blanquists numbered about 2,500 members in Paris, mainly among the Republican youth.[1]

The other current of communist ideas had its fountainhead in the " International " which Caesar de-Paepe, Marx and Bakounine succeeded in winning over to their collectivist ideas. The congresses of the " Association " in Brussels in 1868 and in Bâle in 1869 adopted resolutions of a collectivist character, and many members of the French section were won over to the new ideas.[2]

The success of the " International " in France in 1869 was the sudden result of the strike-movement which swept the country during the last years of the Second Empire. The members of the " International " succeeded in obtaining financial support for some strikers. This raised the prestige of the " Association ", and a number of syndicats sent in their collective adhesion. It is estimated that toward the end of 1869 the " International " had a membership of about 250,000 in France.

These facts had their influence on the French leaders of the " International ". They changed their attitude toward the strike, declaring it " the means *par excellence* for the organization of the revolutionary forces of labor ".[3] The idea of the general strike suggested itself to others.[4] At

---

[1] A. Thomas, *op. cit.*, p. 332.

[2] E. E. Fribourg, *L'Association Internationale des Travailleurs* (Paris, 1871).

[3] A. Thomas, *op. cit.*, p. 363.   [4] *Ibid.*, p. 358.

the Congress of Bâle in 1869, one of the French delegates advocated the necessity of organizing syndicats for two reasons: first, because " they are the means of resisting the exploitation of capital in the present;" and second, because " the grouping of different trades in the city will form the commune of the future " . . . and then . . . " the government will be replaced by federated councils of syndicats and by a committee of their respective delegates regulating the relations of labor—this taking the place of politics." [1]

Under the influence of the " International " the syndicats of Paris,—there were about 70 during the years 1868-1870—founded a local federation under the name of *Chambre Fédérale des sociétés ouvrières de Paris*. This federation formulated its aim in the following terms:

This agreement has for its object to put into operation the means recognized as just by the workingmen of all trades for the purpose of making them the possessors of all the instruments of production and to lend them money, in order that they may free themselves from the arbitrariness of the employer and from the exigencies of capital. . . . The federation has also the aim of assuring to all adhering societies on strike the moral and material support of the other groups by means of loans at the risk of the loaning societies.[2]

These organizations were entirely swept away by the events of 1870-71: the Franco-Prussian War, the Proclamation of the Republic, and especially the Commune. After 1871 the workingmen had to begin the work of organization all over again. But the conquests of the previous period were not lost. The right to strike was recognized. The policy of tolerating workingmen's organiza-

[1] James Guillaume, *L'Internationale, Documents et Souvenirs* (Paris, 1905), vol. i, p. 205.

[2] A. Thomas, *op. cit.*, p. 352.

tions was continued, notwithstanding a few acts to the contrary. But, above all, the experience of the working-men was preserved. The form of organization which they generally advocated after the Commune was the syndicat. The other forms (*i. e.*, the *Compagnonnages* and the secret *Société de résistance*) either disappeared or developed independently along different lines, as the friendly societies.

In other respects, the continuity of the labor movement after the Commune with that of the preceding period was no less evident. As will be seen in the following chapter the problems raised and the solutions given to them by the French workingmen for some time after the Commune were directly related to the movement of the Second Empire. The idea of co-operation, the *mutuellisme* of Proudhon, and the collectivism of the " International " reappeared in the labor movement under the Third Republic.

CHAPTER II

Origin of the General Confederation of Labor
(1872-1895)

THE vigorous suppression of the Commune and the political events which followed it threw the French workingmen for some time into a state of mental depression. Though trade-union meetings were not prohibited, the workingmen avoided the places which had been centers of syndical activity before the Commune. Full of suspicion and fear, they preferred to remain in isolation rather than to risk the persecution of the government.

Under these conditions, the initiative in reconstituting the syndicats was taken by a republican journalist, Barberet.[1] [Barberet was prompted to undertake this "honorable task" by the desire to do away with strikes. He had observed the strike movement for some years, and had come to the conclusion that strikes were fatal to the workingmen and dangerous to the political institutions of the country. His observations had convinced him that the Second Empire had fallen largely in consequence of the strike movement during 1868-70, and he was anxious to preserve the Republic from similar troubles. As he expressed it, strikes were "a crime of *lèse-democratie*"[2] which it was necessary to prevent by all means.

---

[1] Barberet was afterwards appointed chief of the Bureau of Trade Unions, which was constituted as part of the Dept. of the Interior.

[2] J. Barberet, *Monographies Professionelles* (Paris, 1886), vol. i, p. 16.

Barberet outlined the following program for the syndicats. They were to watch over the loyal fulfilment of contracts of apprenticeship; to organize employment bureaus;
to create boards of conciliation composed of an equal number of delegates from employers and from workingmen
for the peaceful solution of trade disputes; to found
libraries and courses in technical education; to utilize their
funds not to " foment strikes ", but to buy raw materials
and instruments of labor; and finally, " to crown these
various preparatory steps " by the creation of co-operative workshops " which alone would give groups of workingmen the normal access to industry and to commerce "
and which would in time equalize wealth.[1]

Under Barberet's influence and with his assistance syndicats were reconstituted in a few trades in Paris during
1872. These syndicats felt the necessity of uniting into a
larger body, and in August of the same year they founded
the *Cercle de l'Union Ouvrière*, which was to form a counter-balance to the employers' organization *L'Union Nation-
ale du Commerce et de l'Industrie*. The *Cercle* insisted on
its peaceful intentions; it declared that its aim was "to
realize concord and justice through study " and to con-
vince public opinion " of the moderation with which the
workingmen claim their rights." [2] The *Cercle* was nevertheless dissolved by the government.

The syndicats, however, were left alone. They slowly
increased in numbers and spread to new trades. There
were about 135 in Paris in 1875. Following the example
of the syndicats of the Second Empire, they organized delegations of workingmen to the Exhibitions of Vienna in
1873 and of Philadelphia in 1876. But their supreme

---

[1] Barberet, *op. cit.*, pp. 20-25.

[2] Fernand Pelloutier, *Histoire des Bourses du Travail* (Paris, 1902),
p. 35.

effort was the organization of the first French Labor Congress in Paris in 1876.

The Congress was attended by 255 delegates from Paris and 105 from the provincial towns. The delegates represented syndicats, co-operative societies and mutual aid societies. The program of the Congress included eight subjects: (1) The work of women; (2) syndical chambers; (3) councils of *prud'hommes;* (4) apprenticeship and technical education; (5) direct representation of the working class in Parliament; (6) co-operative associations of production, of consumption and of credit; (7) old-age pensions; (8) agricultural associations and the relations between agricultural and industrial workers.

The proceedings of the Congress were calm and moderate. The organizers of the Congress were anxious not to arouse the apprehension of the government and not to compromise the republicans with whose help the Congress was organized. The reports and the discussions of the Congress showed that the syndical program outlined by Barberet was accepted by almost all the delegates. They insisted upon the necessity of solving peaceably all industrial difficulties, expressed antipathy for the strike and above all affirmed their belief in the emancipating efficacy of co-operation. At the same time they repudiated socialism, which one of the delegates proclaimed "a bourgeois Utopia".[1]

The syndicats held a second congress in 1876 in Lyons. The Congress of Lyons considered the same questions as did that of Paris, and gave them the same solutions. In general, the character of the second congress was like that of the first.

The third Labor Congress held in Marseilles in 1879, was

[1] *Séances du Congrès Ouvrier de France*, Session de 1876, p. 43.

a new departure in the history of the French labor movement. It marked the end of the influence of Barberet and of the " co-operators " and the beginning of socialist influence. The Congress of Marseilles accepted the title of " Socialist Labor Congress ", expressed itself in favor of the collective appropriation of the means of production and adopted a resolution to organize a workingmen's social political party.

This change in views was brought about by a concurrence of many circumstances. The moderate character of the syndicats between 1872-1879 had been due in large measure to the political conditions of France. The cause of the Republic was in danger and the workingmen were cautious not to increase its difficulties. But after the elections of 1876 and 1877 and upon the election of Grevy to the Presidency, the Republic was more or less securely established, and the workingmen thought that they should now be more outspoken in their economic demands. The Committee which had organized the Congress of Paris had formulated these sentiments in the following terms: "From the moment that the republican form of government was secured ", wrote the Committee, " it was indispensable for the working class, who up to that time had gone hand in hand with the republican bourgeoisie, to affirm their own interests and to seek the means which would permit them to transform their economic condition." [1] It was believed that the means to accomplish this task was co-operation. The belief in co-operation was so intense and general at that time that one of the delegates to the Congress of Paris, M. Finance,[2] himself an opponent of co-operation, predicted a large co-operative movement similar to the move-

[1] *Séances du Congrès Ouvrier*, 1876 (Paris, 1877), p. 9.

[2] Afterward one of the active members of the *Office du Travail*.

ments of 1848-50 and 1864-67. The prediction did not
come true. Nothing important was accomplished in this
field, and the hopes in co-operation receded before the impossibility of putting the idea into practice. The critics
and opponents of co-operation did the rest to discredit the
idea. But when the idea of co-operation lost its influence
over the syndicats, the ground was cleared for socialism.
The Congress of Lyons had declared that " the syndicats
must not forget that the wage-system is but a transitory
stage from serfdom to an unnamed state." [1] When the
hope that this unnamed state would be brought about by
co-operation was gone, the " unnamed " state obtained a
name, for the Socialists alone held out to the workingmen
the promise of a new state which would take the place of
the wage system.

On ground thus prepared the Socialists came to sow their
seed. A group of collectivists, inspired by the ideas of the
" International ", had existed in Paris since 1873.[2] But
this group began to attract attention only in 1877 when it
found a leader in Jules Guesde. Jules Guesde is a remark-
able figure in the history of French Socialism and has played
a great part in shaping the movement. He had edited a
paper, *Les Droits de l'Homme*, in Montpelier in 1870-1 and
had expressed his sympathy for the Commune. This cost
him a sentence of five years in prison. He preferred exile,
went to Switzerland, there came into contact with the " International " and was influenced by Marxian ideas.

On his return to France, Jules Guesde became the spokesman and propagandist of Marxian or " scientific socialism ". Fanatical, vigorous, domineering, he soon made
himself the leader of the French collectivists. Towards

[1] *Assoc. Profess.*, vol. i, p. 243.

[2] Terrail-Mermeix, *La France Socialiste* (Paris, 1886), p. 51.

the end of 1877, he founded a weekly, *L'Égalité,* the first number of which outlined the program which the paper intended to defend. "We believe," wrote *L'Égalité,* " with the collectivist school to which almost all serious minds of the working-class of both hemispheres now belong, that the natural and scientific evolution of mankind leads it irresistibly to the collective appropriation of the soil and of the instruments of labor." In order to achieve this end; *L'Égalité* declared it necessary for the proletariat to constitute itself a distinct political party which should pursue the aim of conquering the political power of the State.[1]

The collectivists found a few adherents among the workingmen who actively propagated the new ideas. In 1878, several syndicats of Paris: those of the machinists, joiners, tailors, leather dressers and others, accepted the collectivist program.

The collectivist ideas were given wider publicity and influence by the persecution of the government. In 1878, an international congress of workingmen was to be held in Paris during the International Exhibition. The Congress of Lyons (1878) had appointed a special committee to organize this international congress. Arrangements were being made for the congress, when the government prohibited it.

The more moderate elements of the Committee gave way before the prohibition of the government, but Guesde and his followers accepted the challenge of the government and continued the preparations for the Congress. The government dispersed the Congress at its very first session and instituted legal proceedings against Guesde and other delegates.

The trial made a sensation and widely circulated the

---

[1] *L'Egalité,* 18 Nov., 1877.

ideas which Guesde defended before the tribunal. From the prison where they were incarcerated the collectivists launched an appeal " to the proletarians, peasant proprietors and small masters " which contained an exposition of collectivist principles and proposed the formation of a distinct political party. The appeal gained many adherents from various parts of France.[1]

The idea of having workingmen's representatives in Parliament had already come up at the Congress of Paris (1876). This Congress, as indicated above, had on its program the question of the " Representation of the Proletariat in Parliament." The reports on this question read at the Congress were extremely interesting. The " moderate co-operators " and " Barberetists ", as they were nicknamed by the revolutionary collectivists, insisted in these reports upon the separation which existed between bourgois and workingmen, upon the inability of the former to understand the interests and the aspirations of the latter, and upon the consequent necessity of having workingmen's representatives in Parliament. These reports revealed the deep-seated sentiments of the workingmen which made it possible for the ideas of class and class struggle to spread among them.

The Congress of Lyons (1878) had advanced the question a step further. It had adopted a resolution that journals should be created which should support workingmen-candidates only.

With all this ground prepared, the triumph of the Socialists at the Congress of Marseilles (1879) was not so sudden as some have thought it to be. The influences which had brought about this change in sentiment were clearly outlined by the Committee on Organization, as may be seen from the following extract:

[1] Terrail-Mermeix, *op. cit.*, p. 98.

From the contact of workingmen-delegates from all civilized nations that had appointed a rendezvous at the International Exhibition, a clearly revolutionary idea disentangled itself. . . . When the International Congress was brutally dispersed by the government, one thing was proven: the working class had no longer to expect its salvation from anybody but itself. . . . The suspicions of the government with regard to the organizers of the Congress, the iniquitous proceedings which it instituted against them, have led to the revolutionary resolutions of the Congress which show that the French proletariat is self-conscious and is worthy of emancipation.[1]

To a similar conclusion had come the Committee on Resolutions appointed by the Congress of Lyons. In the intervals between the two Congresses, it had a conference with the deputies of the Department of Rhone and could report only failure. The deputies, one of whom belonged to the Extreme Left, were against the limitation of hours of work in the name of liberty, and against the liberty of association in the name of the superior rights of the State. " The remedy to this state of affairs," concluded the Committee, " is to create in France a workingmen's party such as exists already in several neighboring states." [1]

The Congress of Marseilles carried out the task which the collectivists assigned to it. A resolution was adopted declaring that the co-operative societies could by no means be considered a sufficiently powerful means for accomplishing the emancipation of the proletariat. Another declared the aim of the Congress to be: " The collectivity of soil and of subsoil, of instruments of labor, of raw materials—to be given to all and to be rendered inalienable by society to whom

[1] Leon Blum, *Les Congrès Ouvriers et Socialistes Français* (Paris, 1901), pp. 33-4.

[2] *Ibid.*, p. 36.

they must be returned." [1] This resolution was adopted by 73 votes against 23.

The Congress also constituted itself a distinct party under the name of the " Federation of Socialist Working-men of France ". The party was organized on a federalist principle. France was divided into six regions: (1) Center or Paris; (2) East or Lyons; (3) Marseilles or South; (4) Bordeaux or West; (5) North or Lille; (6) Algeria. Each region was to have its regional committee and regional congress and be autonomous in its administration. A general committee was to be appointed by the Congress of the Federation, to be held annually in each of the principal regional towns in turn.

After the Congress of Marseilles (1879) the leadership of the syndical movement passed to the Socialists. This led to a split at the next Congress held in Havre in 1880. The " moderates " and " co-operators " separated from the revolutionary collectivists. The former grouped themselves about *L'Union des Chambres Syndicales Ouvrières de France*. They held two separate congresses of their own in 1881 and 1882, which attracted little attention and were of no importance. The *Union des Chambres Syndicales* confined itself to obtaining a reform of the law on syndicats.

The Collectivists themselves, however, were not long united. The movement was soon disrupted by internal divisions and factions. At the Congress of Marseilles (1879) the triumph of collectivism was assured by elements which had the principles of collectivism in common, but which differed in other points. In Havre (1880) these elements were still united against the "moderate" elements. But after the Congress of Havre they separated more and more into distinct and warring groups.

[1] Leon de Seilhac, *Les Congrès Ouvriers en France* (Paris, 1899), p. 47.

The first differentiation took place between the parliamentary socialists on the one hand, and the communist-anarchists on the other. Both divisions had a common aim; the collective appropriation of the means of production. They did not differ much in their ideas on distribution; there were communists among the parliamentary socialists. What separated them most was difference in method. The anarchists rejected the idea that the State, which in their view was and always had been an instrument of exploitation, could ever become an instrument of emancipation, even in the hands of a socialist government. The first act in the Social Revolution, in their opinion, had to be the destruction of the State. With this aim in view, the anarchists wished to have nothing to do with parliamentary politics. They denounced parliamentary action as a " pell-mell of compromise, of corruption, of charlatanism and of absurdities, which does no constructive work, while it destroys character and kills the revolutionary spirit by holding the masses under a fatal illusion."[1] The anarchists saw only one way of bringing about the emancipation of the working-class; namely, to carry on an active propaganda and agitation, to organize groups, and at an opportune moment to raise the people in revolt against the State and the propertied classes; then destroy the State, expropriate the capitalist class and reorganize society on communist and federalist principles. This was the Social Revolution they preached.[2]

From 1883 onward the anarchist propaganda met with success in various parts of France, particularly in Paris

---

[1] *Pourquoi Guesde n'est-il pas anarchiste?* p. 6.

[2] On the anarchist theory, the works of Bakounin, Kropotkin, Reclus and J. Grave should be consulted; on anarchism in France see Dubois, *Le Péril anarchiste;* Garin, *l'Anarchie;* also various periodicals, particularly, *Le Révolte* and *Les Temps Nouveaux.*

and in the South. There were thousands of workingmen who professed the anarchist ideas, and the success of the anarchists was quite disquieting to the socialists.[1]

The socialists, on the contrary, called upon the working-men to participate in the parliamentary life of the country. Political abstention, they asserted, is neither helpful nor possible.[2] The workingman believes in using his right to vote, and to ignore his attitude of mind is of no avail. Besides, to bring about the transformation of capitalist society into a collectivist society, the political machinery of the State must be used. There is no other way of accomplishing this task. The State will disappear after the socialist society has been firmly established. But there is an inevitable transitory period when the main economic reforms must be carried out and during which the political power of the State must be in the hands of the socialist party representing the working-class. The first act of the Social Revolution, therefore, is to conquer the political power of the State.[3]

Within the socialist ranks themselves further divisions soon took place. In 1882, at the Congress of St. Etienne, the party was split into two parts; one part followed Guesde, the other followed Paul Brousse. The latter part took the name of *Parti ouvrier socialiste révolutionnaire français*—it dropped the word "*révolutionnaire*" from its title in 1883—and continued to bear as sub-title, the name "Federation of socialist workingmen of France." Guesde's party took the name of *Parti Ouvrier Français*.

The *Parti Ouvrier Français* claimed to represent the "revolutionary" and "scientific" socialism of Marx. It

---

[1] John Labusquière, *La Troisième République* (Paris), p. 257.

[2] *L'Égalité*, 30 June, 1880.

[3] In socialist writings this transition period is always spoken of as the "Dictatorship of the Proletariat."

accepted the familiar doctrines of "orthodox" Marxism, which it popularized in France. It affirmed its revolutionary character by denying the possibility of reforms in capitalist society and by insisting upon the necessity of seizing the political power of the State in a revolutionary way.

In 1886 J. Guesde wrote as follows:

In the capitalist régime, that is, as long as the means of production and of existence are the exclusive property of a few who work less and less, all rights which the constitutions and the codes may grant to others, to those who concentrate within themselves more and more all muscular and cerebral work, will remain always and inevitably a dead letter. In multiplying reforms, one only multiplies shams (*trompe-l'oeil*).[1]

Inability to carry out real reforms was ascribed to both national legislative bodies and to the municipalities. Therefore,

if the party has entered into elections, it is not for the purpose of carving out seats of councillors or deputies, which it leaves to the hemorroids of bourgeois of every stamp, but because the electoral period brings under our educational influence that part of the masses which in ordinary times is most indifferent to our meetings.[2]

The municipalities conquered were to become just so many centres of recruiting and of struggle. The *Parti Ouvrier* was to be a "kind of recruiting and instructing sergeant preparing the masses for the final assault upon the State which is the citadel of capitalist society."[3] For only a revolution would permit the productive class to seize

---

[1] Jules Guesde, *Le Socialisme au jour le jour* (Paris, 1899), p. 268.

[2] Jules Guesde and Paul Lafargue, *Le Programme du Parti Ouvrier*, 4th edition (Paris, 1897), p. 32.

[3] *Le Programme du Parti Ouvrier*, p. 52.

the political power and to use it for the economic expropriation of capitalistic France and for the nationalization
or socialization of the productive forces. Of course no
man and no party can call forth a revolution, but when
the revolution which the nineteenth century carried within
itself arose as a result of national and international com-
plications, the *Parti Ouvrier* would be the party to assume
the rôle of directing it.[1]

The *Parti Ouvrier* adopted a centralized form of organization. It became in time the strongest and best organized
socialist party of France. It was particularly strong in
the *Department du Nord* and among the textile workers.
It was also known as the " Guesdist " party, after its leader
Guesde.

The *Parti Ouvrier* denounced the members of the *Parti
Ouvrier révolutionnaire socialiste,* or " Broussists," also
thus named after their leader Brousse, as "opportunists and
possibilists " because they believed in the possibility of reforms and had said that it was necessary " to split up our
program until we make it finally possible." [2]   The nick-
name, *possibilists,* has remained as another designation of
the *Broussists.*

The *Broussists* cared little for the theories of Marx.
They were disposed to allow larger differences of doctrine
within their ranks and more local autonomy in their organization. They ascribed much importance to municipal
politics. They conceived the conquest of political power as
a more peaceful process of a gradual infiltration into the
municipal, departmental and national legislative bodies.
But like the " Guesdists," they were collectivists and took
the class struggle as their point of departure.

[1] *Le Programme du Parti Ouvrier,* p. 30.

[2] L. Blum, *op. cit.,* p. 75.

From the very outset, the *Broussists* concentrated their efforts upon gaining an entrance into Parliament and into the municipalities. They had a numerous following in Paris among the working population, and among the lower strata of the middle class.

The split between *Guesdists* and *Broussists* was followed by another in the ranks of the latter. In 1887 the *Broussists* succeeded in electing seven of their members to the municipal council of Paris. This led to internal difficulties. A number of party members were discontented with the organization which they claimed was entirely "bossed" by its leaders. They grouped themselves in their turn about J. Allemane and became known as "Allemanists." The Allemanists accused the Broussists of being too much absorbed in politics and of neglecting the propaganda and organization of the party. In 1890 they separated from the Broussists and constituted a socialist party of their own. The Allemanists absorbed the more revolutionary elements of the party and were the leading spirits in some of the largest and strongest syndicats.

Two more socialist groups must be mentioned in order that the reader may have a complete view of the socialist world in which the syndicats of France were moving during this period. These two were the Blanquists and the Independent Socialists.

The Blanquists—known also as the *Comité Révolutionnaire Central*—were held together by a bond of common tradition, namely, by their loyalty to the name of Blanqui, spoken of in the preceding chapter. The leaders of the Blanquists were men who had taken a more or less prominent part in the Commune and who had returned to France after amnesty was granted in 1880. They considered themselves the heirs of Blanqui and the continuators of his ideas; but under the political conditions of the Third Republic they brushed aside the secret practices of former times and entered into politics as a distinct party with a communist program. Their aim was also the conquest of all political power for the purpose of realizing a communistic society and they approved of all means that would bring about the realization of this end.

The group of Independent Socialists grew out of the " Society for Social Economy " founded in 1885 by Malon, once a member of the " International ". The " Society for Social Economy " was organized for the purpose of elaborating legislative projects of a general socialist character which were published in the monthly of the Society, *La Revue Socialiste.*[1] But the Society soon gained adherents among advanced Republicans and Radicals and entered into politics. It advocated the gradual nationalization of public services, laws for the protection of labor, self-government for the communes, etc. The party became an important factor in the political life of France. Some of the best known socialists of France have come from its ranks, as J. Jaurès, Millerand, Viviani and others.

Amid these socialist factions, the syndicats were a coveted bit torn to pieces because everybody wanted the larger part of it. At their Congress of Paris (1883) the "Broussists " adopted a resolution that " the members of the Party will be bound to enter their syndical chamber or respective trade group and to promote the creation of syndical chambers and of trade groups where none exist as yet." [2] The Guesdists in their turn had adopted a similar resolution at their Congress in Roanne in 1882, and at their succeeding Congress, in Roubaix (1884), they adopted a

[1] On the socialist groups of this period see Leon de Seilhac, *Le Monde Socialiste* (Paris, 1896).

[2] Seilhac, *Les Congrès Ouvriers*, p. 124.

resolution to promote "as soon as possible the formation
of national federations of trades which should rescue the
isolated syndicats from their fatal weakness." [1]   When the
Allemanists separated from the Broussists, they, in their
turn, made it obligatory for members of their party to belong to their respective syndicats.

These acts, while promoting the organization of the syndicats, impressed upon the latter a political character.   The
syndicats were utilized for electoral purposes, were made to
serve the interests of the socialist group to which they adhered, and were drawn into the whirlpool of political dissensions and rivalry.   The effect was destructive for the
syndicats.   The acrimonious and personal polemics of the
socialist leaders bred ill-feeling among their workingmen
followers; the invective and abuse filling the periodical literature of the socialist groups found an echo in the assemblies
of the workingmen; the mutual hatreds separating politi-
cally Allemanists from Guesdists, Guesdists from anarchists
were carried over into the syndicats which were hindered
thereby in their growth or entirely driven to disintegration.
The adherence of a syndicat to any one socialist group
generally repelled the non-socialists and enraged the adherents of other socialist groups, and often led to the organization of rival syndicats in the same trade and locality.
The literature of the French labor movement is full of instances of the disorganizing effect which these political dissensions exerted upon the syndicats.

Economic conditions, however, were impelling the workingmen to union.   Since the Commune, the industrial development of France had gone on without interruption,
concentrating the economic powers of the employing
classes.   In the face of the economic organizations of the

---

[1] Blum, *op. cit.*, p. 93.

employers, the scattered and isolated syndicats were of little significance, and the necessity of a larger combination made itself felt. Besides, in 1884, a new law on syndicats was passed. This law authorized the formation of syndicats under certain conditions of which article 4 was obnoxious to the workingmen. This article 4 of the new law made it obligatory for every syndicat to send in the names and addresses of its administrators to the municipal authorities. In Paris they had to be sent to the Prefect of the Police. The workingmen thought that this condition would subject them to the mercy of the police and of the employers, and they wanted to manifest their attitude to the new law.

Under these conditions a general congress of syndicats was called in Lyons in October, 1886. Organized workingmen of various political opinions met here and at once the sentiments and needs which brought them together found expression in the report of the Committee on Organization from which the following lines may be quoted:

We are organized workingmen who have made a study of social problems and who have recognized that the diversity of doctrines contributes powerfully to divide us instead of uniting us.

Slaves of the same master, bearing the same claims, suffering from the same evils, having the same aspirations, the same needs and the same rights, we have decided to set aside our political and other preferences, to march hand in hand, and to combine our forces against the common enemy. The problems of labor have always the power of uniting the workingmen.[1]

The first question on the program of the Congress was the " prospect of a Federation of all workingmen's syndi-

---

[1] *Séances du Congrès Ouvrier*, session de 1886, pp. 18-19.

cats." The discussion brought out the fact that the delegates had different ideas on the future rôle of the Federation. Still the majority united on the following resolution:

Considering that in face of the powerful bourgeois organization made without and against the working-class, it not only behooves, but it is the duty of the latter to create, by all means possible, groupings and organizations of workingmen against those of the bourgeois, for defense first, and we hope for offensive action soon afterwards;

Considering that every organization of workingmen which is not imbued with the distinction of classes, by the very fact of the economic and political conditions of existing society, and which exist only for the sake of giving assent to the will of the government and of the bourgeoisie, or of presenting petty observations of a respectful and therefore of a humiliating nature for the dignity of the working-class, cannot be considered as part of the workingmen's armies marching to the conquest of their rights; for these reasons,

A National Federation is founded. . . .[1]

The aim of the Federation was to help individual syndicats in their struggles with employers.

"The National Federation of Syndicats," however, did not achieve its end. It soon fell into the hands of the Guesdists who utilized the organization for political and electoral purposes. The Congresses of the " National Federation of Syndicats" were held in the same place and about the same time as were those of the *Parti Ouvrier,* were composed of the same men and passed the same resolutions. Besides, the " National Federation of Syndicats " never . succeeded in establishing connections between the local syndicats and the central organization (the *Counseil*

---

[1] *Congrès National des Syndicats Ouvriers, Compte Rendu,* pp. 344-5.

fédéral national) and could, therefore, exert little economic influence.

While the " National Federation of Syndicats " became a war-engine at the service of the Guesdists,[1] another central organization was created by the rivals of the Guesdists. This was the " Federation of Labor Exchanges of France " (*Fédération des Bourses du Travail de France*). The idea of the *Bourse du Travail* may be traced back to the middle of the nineteenth century and even further back to the Great Revolution.[2] At first the idea was to erect a building where the workingmen in need of work and the employers in need of workingmen could meet. It was proposed that the prevailing rate of wages in each industry be published there day by day and that the quotations of the *Bourse du Travail* then be inserted in the newspapers. . . . It was expected that the workingmen of an entire country, even of an entire continent would be enabled in this manner to know, day by day, the places where work might be obtained under the most favorable conditions, and where they might choose to go to demand it.[3] But after the law of 1884 which legalized the syndicats, the *Bourse du Travail* was conceived in a larger spirit, as a center where all the syndicats of a locality could have their headquarters, arrange meetings, give out information, serve as bureaus of employment, organize educational courses, have their libraries and bring the workingmen of all trades into contact with one another. The municipalities were to promote their creation and to subsidize them.[4]

---

[1] Pelloutier, *op. cit.*, p. 60.

[2] Charles Franck, *Les Bourses du Travail et la Confédération Générale du Travail* (Paris, 1910), p. 17.

[3] G. de Molinari, *Les Bourses du Travail* (Paris, 1893), p. 257.

[4] Molinari, *op. cit.*, p. 280.

The first *Bourse du Travail* was opened in Paris in 1887. The example of Paris was followed by other municipalities of France, and in a short time many of the larger cities of France had their *Bourses du Travail*. The Allemanists obtained the predominating influence in the *Bourses du Travail*, and they conceived the idea of opposing to the " National Federation of Syndicats "—which was an instrument in the hands of the Guesdists—a " Federation of *Bourses du Travail*," in which they would have the leading part. [1] The " Federation of *Bourses du Travail* " was organized in 1892 with the following program: (1) To unify the demands of the workingmen's syndicats and to bring about the realization of these demands; (2) To extend and to propagate the action of the *Bourses du Travail*, in the industrial and agricultural centers; (3) To nominate delegates to the National Secretariat of Labor; (4) To collect statistical data and to communicate them to the adhering Bourses, and at the same time to generalize the gratuitous service of finding employment for workers of both sexes and of all trades. [2]

The " National Secretariat of Labor " mentioned was created after the International Socialist Congress of Brussels in 1891. The Congress of Brussels had proposed to create in all countries National Secretariats in order to unify the labor and socialist movement of the world. In France, the National Secretariat of Labor soon experienced the fate of other organizations. In view of political differences, it was abandoned by the Guesdists, Independents, and Broussists. It therefore could not achieve the aim it had in view and lost all significance.

Into this situation there now entered another factor,

[1] Pelloutier, *op. cit.*, p. 64.

[2] Seilhac, *Les Congrès Ouvriers*, p. 230.

which was to determine the course of further groupings. This factor was the idea of the general strike. The idea was not new in the history of the labor movement and not original with France. It had been widely discussed in England during the 30's [1] and afterwards at the Congresses of the " International ".[2] It reappeared in France in the second half of the 80's and seems to have been suggested by the wide strike movement in America during 1886-7. Its first propagandist in France seems to have been a French anarchist workingman, Tortelier, a member of the syndicat of carpenters.[3]

The idea of the general strike was hailed enthusiastically by the French syndicats. On the one hand it seemed to give the workingmen a new weapon in their economic struggles. It was seen above how reluctant French workingmen had been to use the strike during the 60's and 70's. Though forced by economic conditions to use it, the French workingmen still considered it a necessary evil which never fully rewarded the sacrifices it involved. The general strike seemed to repair the defects of the partial strike. It seemed to insure success by increasing the number of strikers and by extending the field of disturbance. On the other hand, the general strike suggested itself as a method of bringing about the Social Revolution. This question was a vital one with the socialist syndicats. It was much debated and discussed and divided deeply the adherents of the various socialist and anarchist groups. " The conquest of political power," the method advocated by Guesdists and others, seemed vague and indefinitely remote; a general re-

---

[1] B. & S. Webb, *History of Trade Unionism*, pp. 118-122.

[2] Dr. E. Georgi, *Theorie und Praxis des Generalstreiks in der modernen Arbeiter-bewegung* (Jena, 1908).

[3] H. Lagardelle, *La Grève Générale et le Socialisme* (Paris, 1905), p. 42.

volt, such as advocated by the anarchists, seemed impossible in view of the new armaments and of the new construction of cities which made barricades and street fighting a thing of the past. These two methods eliminated, the general strike seemed to present the only and proper weapon in the hands of the workingmen for the realization of their final emancipation.

In this sense, the principle of the general strike was voted for the first time in 1888 at the Congress of the " National Federation of Syndicats " in Bordeaux. The idea spread rapidly. The Allemanists declared in favor of it at their Congresses in 1891 and 1892.[1] Fernand Pelloutier, of whom more will be said in the next chapter, defended it successfully before a socialist congress in Tours in 1892. The same year, Aristide Briand appeared as the eloquent champion of the general strike before the Congress of the " National Federation of Syndicats " in Marseilles.[2] The Blanquists admitted the general strike as one of the possible revolutionary means. Only the Guesdists were against the general strike and at their Congress in Lille (1890) declared it impossible.

The conception of the general strike that prevailed during this period was that of a peaceful cessation of work. The strike, it was agreed, is a right guaranteed by law. Even if a strike were to spread to many industries and assume a general character, the workingmen would still be exercising their rights and could not be lawfully prosecuted. The general strike, therefore, would enable the workingmen to carry out a Revolution by legal means and would make the revolution an easy matter. The general strike must mean revolution because a complete cessation of work

[1] L. Blum, *op. cit.*, pp. 129, 137.

[2] *Le Congrès National des Syndicats, Compte Rendu*, pp. 15 *et seq.*

would paralyze the life of the country and would reduce
the ruling classes to famine. Lasting a few days only, it
would compel the government to capitulate before the workingmen, and would carry the workingmen's party into
power. Thus, a " peaceful strike of folded arms " (*grève
des bras croisés*) would usher in the Social Revolution
which would bring about the transformation of society.
The feeling prevailed that the general strike could begin
any moment and that it assured the speedy realization of
the socialist ideal. At first it was thought that the general
strike could be organized or decreed, but this idea was soon
given up, and the general strike came to be thought of as
a spontaneous movement which might be hastened only by
propaganda and organization.

The conception of the general strike involved one more
important point. It implied the superior value of the economic method of organization and struggle over the political. The general strike is a phenomenon of economic life
and must be based on an economic organization of the
working-class.

On this conception of the general strike the Guesdists
threw themselves with all the subtlety of their dialectics.
They asserted that the idyllic picture of the social revolution was too puerile to be taken seriously; that before the
capitalists felt the pangs of hunger, the workingmen would
already have starved.[1] They insisted that no such peaceful
general strike was possible; that either the workingmen
would lose their composure, or the government would pro-
voke a collision. On the other hand, they affirmed that a
successful general strike presupposes a degree of organiza-

---

[1] To meet this criticism the Allemanists argued that the militant
workingmen could have " reserves " accumulated little by little which
would allow them to await for some time the results of the general
strike.

tion and solidarity among workingmen which, if realized, would make the general strike itself unnecessary. But, above all, they argued that the general strike could be successful, because in the economic field the workingmen are weaker than the capitalists and cannot hope to win; that only in the political field are the workingmen equal, and even superior to the employers, because they are the greater number. The conclusion, therefore, was that "the general strike is general nonsense" and that the only hope of the workingmen lay in the conquest of political power. The syndicat could only have a secondary and limited importance in the struggle for emancipation.[1]

The attitude of the Guesdists towards the general strike brought them into conflict with the "National Federation of Syndicats" which voted in favor of the general strike at Marseilles in 1892. The conflict at first was latent, but soon led to a split in the "National Federation of Syndicats" and to a readjustment of the various elements of the syndicats. This took place in the following way.

In 1893 the *Bourse du Travail* of Paris was authorized by the Second Congress of the "Federation of Bourses" to call a general trade-union Congress in which all syndicats should take part. The Congress was to convene the 18th of July, 1893. About ten days before this, the government closed the *Bourse du Travail* of Paris. The reason given was that the syndicats adhering to the Bourse had not conformed to the law of 1884. This act of the government provoked an agitation among the workingmen, the Congress took on a character of protest, and a large number of syndicats wished to be represented.

The Congress of Paris adopted the principle of the gen-

---

[1] G. Deville, *Principes Socialistes* (Paris, 1896), pp. 191-201.

eral strike by vote, but in view of governmental persecution, the necessity of unifying the forces of the workingmen was thought to ·be the most important question. It
was discussed at length, and the Congress adopted a resolution, that all existing syndicats, within the shortest
possible time, should join the Federation of their trade or
constitute such a federation if none as yet existed; that
they should form themselves into local federations or
Bourses du Travail and that these Federations and
Bourses du Travail should form a " National Federation,"
and the Congress invited the " Federation of Bourses du
Travail " and the " National Federation of Syndicats " to
merge into one organization.

The Congress of Paris also called a general Congress of
syndicats for the following year in Nantes and commis-
sioned the *Bourse du Travail* of Nantes to arrange the
Congress. The " Bourse " of Nantes had already received
a mandate from the " National Federation of Syndicats "
to arrange its Congress. It therefore decided to arrange
both Congresses at the same time and to make one Congress out of two. The National Council of the " Federation of Syndicats ", where the Guesdists presided, protested, but with no result. A general Congress of syndicats was held in Nantes in 1894.

By this time the number of syndicats in France had considerably increased. According to the *Annuaire Statistique,* the growth of the syndicats since 1884 was as follows:

Year	Number of syndicats	Membership
1884	68	
1885	221	
1886	280	
1887	501	
1888	725	
1889	821	
1890	1,006	139,692
1891	1,250	205,152
1892	1,589	288,770
1893	1,926	402,125
1894	2,178	403,440

Of these, 1,662 syndicats were represented at the Congress of Nantes. This fact shows how keen was the interest felt in the idea of the general strike which, it was known, was to be the main question at the Congress.

The Congress of Nantes adopted a motion in favor of the general strike, appointed a " Committee for the propaganda of the general strike " and authorized this committee to collect 10 per cent of all subscriptions for strikes. The Guesdist delegates after this vote left the Congress and held a separate Congress by themselves.

The majority of the delegates remained and voted the creation of a " National Council " which should form the central organization of all the syndicats of France.

The " National Council " functioned unsatisfactorily. At the next general Congress in Limoges (1895) the " National Council " was abolished and the foundations of a new organization were laid. This new organization was the " General Confederation of Labor ".

The workingmen had come to recognize that political divisions were disastrous to the growth of the syndicats. The elimination of politics from the syndicats was, therefore, adopted at Limoges as a condition of admission to the " General Confederation ". The first article of the Statutes read :

Among the various syndicats and associations of syndicats of workingmen and of employes of both sexes existing in France and in its Colonies, there is hereby created a uniform and collective organization with the name General Confederation of Labor.

The elements constituting the General Confederation of Labor will remain independent of all political schools (*en dehors de toute école politique*).

The aim of the Confederation was evidently formulated to satisfy all conceptions. Its vague wording was as follows: " The General Confederation of Labor has the exclusive purpose of uniting the workingmen, in the economic domain and by bonds of close solidarity, in the struggle for their integral emancipation." [1]

The " General Confederation of Labor " incorporated the general strike as part of its program.

The creation of the " General Confederation of Labor " may be considered the first important manifestation of the revolutionary tendency in the syndical movement of France. As Mr. Leon de Seilhac justly remarks, " the Congress of Limoges was a victory of the syndicalist revolutionary party over the syndicalist party of politics (*Parti syndical politicien*). The victory was on the side of those who hailed the general strike, who asserted the superiority of economic action over political and who wanted to keep the syndicats independent of the political parties. These ideas contained the germ of revolutionary syndicalism and the Allemanists who emphasized them before others may thus be said to have pointed out the lines along which revolutionary syndicalism was to develop.

The " General Confederation of Labor ", however, was not founded by Allemanists alone. Its organization was

---

[1] Seilhac, *Les Congrès Ouvriers*, p. 286.

advocated by Blanquists and non-socialist workingmen. The Blanquists had always insisted upon the necessity of an independent economic organization and had refused to admit syndicats into their political organizations as constituent elements. The non-socialist workingmen, on the other hand, contributed to the foundation of the " General Confederation " because they felt the economic importance of a central syndical organization.

The " General Confederation of Labor " took the place of the " National Federation of Syndicats ". The Guesdists that had split off at the Congress of Nantes continued for some time to bear the title of " National Federation of Syndicats ", but their organization was of no importance and was soon lost in the general organization of the *Parti Ouvrier*.

The " National Secretariat of Labor " died a quiet death (in 1896), after having expended the little energy it had. There were, therefore, now two central organizations: (1) The General Confederation of Labor, and (2) The Federation of Bourses du Travail. In these the further history of syndicalism centers.

CHAPTER III

THE FEDERATION OF BOURSES DU TRAVAIL. (1892-1902)

THE *Bourses du Travail* met an important want in the syndical life of France. The local syndicats were generally poor and could accomplish but little in their isolation. The *Bourse du Travail* furnished them with a center where they could easily come to a common understanding and plan common action.

The first *Bourse du Travail*, as indicated above, was opened by the Municipal Council of Paris in 1887. In 1892 there were already fourteen Bourses in existence. Their number increased as follows:

Year	Bourses du Travail
1894	34
1896	45
1898	55
1899	65
1900	75
1902	96

Outside of Paris, the initiative of creating a *Bourse du Travail* was generally taken by the workingmen themselves. The local syndicats would elect a committee to work out statutes and a table of probable expenses and income. The project of the committee would then be submitted to the general assembly of the syndicats. The assembly would also elect an administrative council, a secretary, treasurer and other officers. The statutes, the list of adhering syndicats, and the names of the administrative officers would then be presented to the municipal authorities, and the

Bourse du Travail, which in fact was a local federation of unions, would be formally constituted.

In many places, local federations existed before 1887. These simply had to assume the new title to transform themselves into *Bourses du Travail.* The municipalities would then intervene and grant a subvention. Up to 1902 inclusive, the municipalities of France spent 3,166,159 francs in installing *Bourses du Travail,* besides giving the annual subventions. In 1902, the subvention received by all the *Bourses du Travail* of France from the municipalities amounted to 197,345 francs, and 48,550 francs besides were contributed to their budget by the Departments.[1] The readiness of the municipal councils to subsidize the *Bourses du Travail* was due mostly, if not always, to political considerations.

Though soliciting subventions from the municipalities, the syndicats insisted on being absolutely independent in the administration of the Bourses. The first Congress of the *Bourses du Travail* in 1892 declared that:

Whereas the *Bourses du Travail* must be absolutely independent in order to render the services which are expected from them;

Whereas this institution constitutes the only reform which the workingmen have wrested from the ruling class;

The Congress of *Bourses du Travail* of 1892 declares that the workingmen must reject absolutely the meddling of the administrative and governmental authorities in the functioning of the Bourses,—an interference which was manifested in the declaration of public utility;

Invites the workingmen to make the most energetic efforts in order to guarantee the entire independence of the *Bourses du Travail,* and to refuse the municipalities if they or the government desire to interfere with their functioning.[2]

[1] *Annuaire Statistique.*

[2] Seilhac, *Congrès Ouvriers,* p. 231.

The municipalities, on the contrary, wanted to have some control over the funds they furnished. The result was more or less friction. In 1894, the Congress of the *Bourses du Travail* decided to demand that the Bourses be declared institutions of public utility; this, it was thought, would put them under the protection of the law and make impossible any hostile act on the part of the administration. But the next year the fourth Congress of the *Bourses du Travail* reversed the decision of the preceding Congress and declared for complete independence.

As the *Bourses du Travail* became more aggressive, the difficulties with regard to the municipalities increased. At the fifth congress of the *Bourses du Travail* 1896) in Tours, a report was presented showing the Bourses how they could exist without the subvention of the municipalities. The question of financial independence was brought up at later Congresses, but received no solution. The Bourses could not live on their own resources, while they continued the activities which brought them now and then into conflict with the municipal authorities.

The program which the *Bourses du Travail* gradually outlined for themselves has been classified under four heads: (1) Benevolent Services, or as the French term it *Mutualité;* (2) *Instruction;* (3) *Propaganda;* and (4) *Resistance.*[1]

The services of *Mutualité* included finding employment for workingmen out of work (*Placement*), assistance to workmen who go from city to city in search of employment (*Viaticum*), aid to other unemployed persons, sick benefit, etc. The Bourses paid particular attention to the

---

[1] On the *Bourses du Travail* see, F. Pelloutier, *Histoire des Bourses du Travail*, 1902; Ch. Franck, *Les Bourses du Travail et la Confédération Générale du Travail*, 1910; P. Delesalle, *Les Bourses du Travail et la C. G. T.* (Paris, 1910).

service of *placement*. Pelloutier, the Secretary of the Federation of Bourses, wrote:

The Placement is in fact the first and greatest advantage which the federative grouping can offer to the workingmen, and it constitutes a powerful instrument of recruiting. In consequence of the instability of employment, the use of private employment buieaus for whose services payment has to be made, soon becomes so onerous that many workingmen exasperated by the necessity of deducting from their future wages (which are more and more reduced) considerable tithes for the services of employment bureaus, prefer often—though losing thereby —to spend their time in search of a place which will secure a livelihood. Besides, it is known—and the proceedings of Parliament have furnished decisive proof—that the habitual practice of the employment bureaus is to procure the most precarious employments so as to multiply the number of visits which the workingmen will have to pay them. It is therefore easy to understand the readiness with which the unfortunates go to the *Bourse du Travail,* which offers desired employment gratuitously. In this manner men who would hold aloof from the syndicats out of ignorance or indifference, enter them under the pressure of need and find there instruction, the utility and importance of which escaped them before.[1]

The services of instruction comprised the founding of libraries, the organization of technical courses, the arrangement of lectures on general subjects (economic, literary, historical, etc.), workingmen's journals, bureaus of information, etc.

The propaganda of the Bourses had for its general aim the intellectual development of the workingman and the extension of the syndical movement. The Bourses were to support the syndicats in existence, organize new ones, promote the adherence of single syndicats to their national

---

[1] Pelloutier, *op. cit.,* pp. 87-88.

federations, carry on a propaganda among the agricultural laborers and perform other functions of a similar character.

The services of resistance consisted in lending material and moral aid to the workingmen in their economic struggles. The Bourses regarded themselves mainly as societies of resistance whose principal function was to support the workingmen in struggle. The other functions were considered subordinate to this main service.

Every Bourse carried out this program only in proportion to its means. The Bourses differed a great deal in number of adherents, in financial resources, in command of organizers, etc. Some consisted of a few syndicats with a few dozen members only; others comprised tens of syndicats with thousands of organized workingmen and with a budget running into the thousands.

A few figures may help to form some idea of the extent of the services rendered by the *Bourses du Travail* during the period considered in this chapter. The number of positions filled by the Bourses were as follows:

Year	Applications for employment	Offers of employment	Placed at residence	Placed away from residence
1895	38,141	17,190	15,031	5,335
1898	83,648	45,461	47,237	38,159
1902	99,330	60,737	44,631	30,544 [1]

The service of *viaticum* was organized differently by different Bourses. Some paid one franc a day, others one and one-half and two francs. In many Bourses the traveling workingmen received part only of the *viaticum* in money, the rest in kind (tickets to restaurants, lodging, etc.). The reports of the Bourses presented to their Congress at Paris in 1900, contain some information on the subject. The Bourse of Alger spent from 600 to 700 francs a year on the service of *viaticum*. The Bourse of

[1] *Annuaire Statistique.*

Bordeaux distributed during certain months about 130 francs, during others, only 60; other Bourses spent much less. The following table presents the amounts spent in successive years by the Bourse of Rennes:

		Assistance	
Year	Passing Workmen	Francs	Centimes
1894 25		37	50
1895 22		33	
1896 47		60	50
1897 41		81	
1898 (till Sept.) 32		64	

In organizing technical courses, the *Bourses du Travail* pursued the aim of fighting "the dominant tendency in modern industry to make of the child a laborer, an unconscious accessory of the machine, instead of making him an intelligent collaborator."[1]   Again in this respect the services of the Bourses varied.   In the Bourse of Etienne, 597 courses of two hours each were attended by 426 pupils from October 1, 1899, to June 30, 1911.   The Bourse of Marseilles had in 1900 courses in carpentry, metallurgy, typography and others.   The Bourse of Toulouse organized 20 courses and had its own typographical shop.

Nearly all Bourses organized their own libraries, some of which consisted of several hundred volumes, while the library of the *Bourse du Travail* of Paris contained over 2,000 volumes.   Besides, every large Bourse had its periodical, weekly or monthly.[2]

The *Fédération des Bourses du Travail* was formed in 1892 to systematize and to unify the activities of the Bourses.   Though it owed its origin to political motives, the Federation soon devoted its main energies to the economic functions of the Bourses which it tried to extend and

[1] Pelloutier, *op. cit.*, pp. 121-2.

[2] There were 23 in 1907.   Franck, *op. cit.*, pp. 127-8.

to strengthen. This turn in its policy the Federation owed chiefly to Fernand Pelloutier, who became secretary of the Federation in 1894 and who remained in this post till his death in 1901.

Fernand Pelloutier (1867-1901) came from a bourgeois family and was educated in a Catholic school.[1] He entered political life at an early age in a provincial town (St. Nazaire), as an advanced republican, but soon passed into the socialist ranks. Though a member of the *Parti Ouvrier* (Guesdists), he defended the general strike in 1892 before a socialist Congress in Tours. This caused his break with the *Parti Ouvrier*. In 1893 he came to Paris and here came under the influence of the Anarchist-Communists, whose ideas he fully accepted and professed to his last day.

Pelloutier was appointed secretary of the Federation of Bourses in order to assure the political neutrality of the organization. As indicated in the previous chapter, the Federation owed its birth largely to the political interests of the Allemanists. The Federation, however, soon found itself composed of various elements—Blanquists, Guesdists, etc. —but the economic interests which stimulated the growth of the Bourses were strong enough to create a desire on the part of the workingmen to avoid political dissensions and quarrels. An anarchist at the head of the Federation seemed to guarantee the necessary neutrality.

Fernand Pelloutier realized the expectations placed in him. He was disgusted with politics and his " dream was to oppose a strong, powerful economic action to political action." [2] The Federation of Bourses became his absorbing interest in life. To it he devoted most of his time and

[1] On the life of Pelloutier see Maurice Pelloutier, *F. Pelloutier. Sa Vie, son Oeuvre* (Paris, 1911).

[2] P. Delessale, *Temps Nouveaux*, 23 Mars, 1901.

energy. He proved himself a man of steady purpose, of
methodical procedure, and of high organizing abilities. He
has been recognized as the most able organizer of the working class that modern France has produced. His services to the development of the syndicalist movement have
been recognized by men of various opinions and political
convictions. M. Seilhac wrote of him in 1897, " a young
man, intelligent, educated, sprung from the bourgeoisie,
has just entered the Federation as Secretary; M. F. Pelloutier has led the Federation with a talent and a surety of
judgment which his most implacable enemies must acknowledge. Having passed through the ' Guesdist ' school, M.
Pelloutier violently broke away from this intolerant and
despotic party and was attracted by pure anarchism. The
Federation owes its rapid success in great measure to
him." [1]

In 1892 the Federation was formed by ten Bourses out
of the fourteen then in existence. Its growth was as follows:

Year	Bourses	Syndicats
1895	34	606
1896	46	862
1897	40	627
1898	51	947
1899	54	981
1900	57	1,061
1902	83	1,112

The Federation was represented by a Federal Committee
in Paris. Each Bourse had the right to a delegate in the
Committee, but a single delegate could represent several
Bourses. As the Federal Committee was in Paris, the dele-
gates were not members of the Bourses they represented.
They were chosen by the Bourses from a list sent to them

[1] Seilhac, Congrès Ouvriers, p. 272.

by the Secretary of the Federation and made up of men either personally known by him or recommended to him. This gave rise to dissatisfaction, and it was decided that the secretary should complete the list of candidates with remarks on their political attachments, so that the Bourses might choose representatives expressing exactly their opinions.

In this way the Federal Committee came to be composed of various political elements. In 1899 there were 48 Bourses in the Federation; of these three were represented in the Federal Committee by Blanquists, eleven by Allemanists, five by Guesdists. The last named soon left the Federation; the rest did not adhere to any party. "Within the group of their representatives particularly," wrote Pelloutier, "must one look for those convinced libertarians [1] whom the Bourses have maintained as delegates regardless of the reproaches of certain socialist schools, and who, without fuss, have done so much for some years to enhance the individual energy and the development of the syndicats." [2] The Committee had no executive officers, not even a chairman. The business was done by the secretary, an assistant secretary and a treasurer. The first received 1,200 francs a year. Each session began with the reading of the minutes of the preceding session, and of the correspondence; then the discussion of the questions raised by the correspondence, inscribed on the order of the day, or raised by the delegates, occurred. A vote took place only in cases, "extremely rare", when an irreconcilable divergence of views sprang up. The meetings took place twice a month.

Pelloutier wrote:

The suppression of the chairmanship and of useless voting

---

[1] The anarchists in France call themselves *libertaires*.

[2] Pelloutier, *op. cit.*, p. 151.

dates only from the entrance of the libertarians into the Committee, but experience soon convinced all members that between serious and disinterested men there is no necessity of a monitor because everyone considers it an honor to respect the freedom of discussion and even, (without wavering from his principles) to conduct the debate in a conversational tone.

The Federal Committee proceeded in a methodical way. Between 1894-1896 it devoted itself mainly to propaganda and to organization. It invited the local syndicats and unions of syndicats to constitute themselves into *Bourses du Travail*. To guide them Pelloutier wrote a little pamphlet on *The method of organizing and maintaining Bourses du Travail*. After 1895 the Federal Committee thought the multiplication of Bourses too rapid. The Committee feared that the Bourses were constituting themselves without sufficient syndical strength and that they were putting themselves at the mercy of a dissolution or of an unsuccessful strike.

The Committee, therefore, thought it wise if not to moderate the organizing enthusiasm of the militant workingmen, at least to call their attention to the utility of extending to arrondissements, sometimes even to an entire department, a propaganda which was till then limited to a local circle. Two or three Bourses per Department, wrote Pelloutier, would group the workingmen more rapidly and at the cost of less efforts than seven or eight insufficiently equipped and necessarily weak.[1]

In 1897, at the Congress of Toulouse, Pelloutier read two reports in which he invited the *Bourses du Travail* to extend their activities to the agricultural population and to the sailors. These reports reveal a thorough study of the conditions in which these two classes of the population

[1] F. Pelloutier, *op. cit.*, p. 77.

spend their lives, and contain indications how to attract them to syndical activity. Pelloutier recommended the Bourses to create commissions which should be specially devoted to agricultural problems and which should train propagandists for the country. He also recommended the institution of homes for sailors in the ports.

Some Bourses acted on the suggestion of Pelloutier and since then dates the propaganda carried on by some Bourses among the wood-cutters, the wine-growers, the agricultural laborers, the fishermen, sailors and similar groups of the working population.

From 1898 to 1900 the Federal Committee was trying to systematize the services of the *placement* and of the *viaticum*. The suggestion came from some Bourses, which particularly felt this necessity. Some Bourses had already been placing workingmen at a distance through correspondence. They wanted to generalize this by having the Federal Committee publish statistics of the fluctuations of employment in the various Bourses. On the other hand, the Bourses had difficulties with the service of *viaticum*. The diversity of conditions in this respect gave rise to dissatisfaction, while the Bourses were unable to control abuses. The secretaries could not know the number of visits paid them by workingmen, nor the amounts received by each.

At the Congress of Rennes (1898), the Federal Committee presented a plan of a " federal viaticum ", and in 1900, the *Office national de statistique et de placement* was organized. The "federal viaticum" was optional for members of the federation, and though presenting certain advantages for the Bourses, was accepted by very few of them. Organized in 1899, it functioned unsatisfactorily.

The *Office national* began activity in June, 1900. It was organized with the financial aid of the government. In 1900, after the Universal Exhibition, Paris was overcrowded with unemployed workingmen, and the government thought it could make use of the Federation of Bourses to disperse them over the country. Before that, in November, 1899, the Federal Committee had addressed the government for a subsidy of 10,000 francs to organize the *Office national*. In June, 1900, the Government granted 5,000 francs. The *Office* began to publish a weekly statistical bulletin containing the information on the fluctuation of employment sent to the Federal Committee by the Bourses. The *Office*, however, did not give the expected results. In organizing these services, the Federation of Bourses always kept in mind the interests of the syndicats. It directed workingmen to employers who satisfied the general conditions imposed by the syndicats. The *viaticum* also served to diminish competition among workingmen in ordinary times, or during strikes.

In all its activity the Federal Committee generally followed the same policy. It called the attention of one Bourse to the experiments and to the achievements of others; it made its own suggestions and recommendations and it carried out the decisions of the Congresses. It did not regard itself as a central organ with power to command. Constituted on a federalist basis, the Bourses expected from the Federal Committee merely the preliminary study of problems of a common interest, reserving for themselves the right to reject both the problems and the study; they considered even their Congresses merely as *foyers* where the instruments of discussion and of work were forged.[1]

The activity of the Federal Committee was handicapped by insufficiency of means. The financial state of the Federation between 1892 and 1902 may be gathered from the following table:

[1] F. Pelloutier, *op. cit.*, p. 154.

	Receipts		Expenses	
	Francs	Centimes	Francs	Centimes
1892-1893	247		209	45
1893-1894	573	95	378	95
1894-1895	1,342	55	960	07
1895-1896	2,380	05	1,979	
1896-1897	2,310	75	1,779	45
1897-1900	6,158	75	5,521	45
1900-1901	4,297	85	3,029	71
1901-1902	5,541—	85	4,320	80

The Bourses paid their dues irregularly and Pelloutier complained that with such means the Committee could not render all the services it was capable of and that it was necessarily reduced to the rôle of a correspondence bureau, " slow and imperfect in its working."

Whatever others may have thought of the results obtained by the Federation of Bourses, the leaders themselves felt enthusiastic about the things accomplished. Pelloutier wrote:

Enumerate the results obtained by the groupings of workingmen; consult the program, of the courses instituted by the *Bourses du Travail,* a program which omits nothing which goes to make up a moral, complete, dignified and satisfied life; regard the authors who inhabit the workingmen's libraries; admire this syndical and co-operative organization which extends from day to day and embraces new categories of producers, the unification of all the proletarian forces into a close network of syndicats, of co-operative societies, of leagues of resistance; consider the constantly increasing intervention into the diverse manifestations of social life; the examination of methods of production and of distribution and say whether this organization, whether this program, this tendency towards the beautiful and the good, whether this aspiration toward the complete expansion of the individual do not justify the pride the Bourses du Travail feel.[1]

---

[1] F. Pelloutier, *op. cit.,* pp. 170-1.

This feeling and the preoccupation with socialist ideals led Pelloutier and other members of the Federation to think that the *Bourses du Travail* could not only render immediate services, but that they were capable of "adapting themselves to a superior social order". Pelloutier thought that the *Bourses du Travail* were evolving from this time on the elements of a new society, that they were gradually constituting a veritable socialist (economic and anarchic) state within the bourgeois state,[1] and that they would in time, substitute communistic forms of production and of distribution for those now in existence. The question was brought up for discussion at the Congress of Tours (1896) and two reports were read on the present and future rôle of the *Bourses du Travail*. One report was written by Pelloutier, the other was prepared by the delegates of the Bourse of Nimes, Claude Gignoux and Victorien Briguier (Allemanists).

The report of the Bourse of Nimes starts out from the idea that no new plan of a future society need be fabricated; that the *Bourses du Travail* show themselves already capable of directing the economic activities of society and that with further growth they will become more and more capable of so doing. The natural development of the Bourses, it held, leads them to investigate the number of unemployed in each trade; the causes of industrial perturbation, the cost of maintenance of each individual in comparison with wages received; the number of trades and of workingmen employed in them; the amount of the produce; the totality of products necessary for the population of their region, etc., etc. Now, it further set forth, with all this information at hand, and with all this economic experience, each Bourse could, in case of a social transformation,

---

[1] F. Pelloutier, *op. cit.*, p. 160.

assume the direction of the industrial life of its region.
Each trade organized in a syndicat would elect a council
of labor; the syndicats of the same trade would be federated nationally and internationally.   The Bourses, knowing
the quantity of products which must be produced, would impart this information to the councils of labor of each trade,
which employ all members of the trade in the manufacture
of necessary products.   By their statistics, the Bourses
would know where there is excess or want of production in
their regions, and would determine the exchange of products between the territories which by nature are adapted
for some special production only.   The report presupposed
that property would become " social and inalienable "; and
the assumption was that the workingmen would be stimulated to develop the industrial powers of their regions and
to increase the material welfare of the country.   The report concluded:

This summary outline gives those who live in the syndical
movement an idea of the rôle which falls and will fall to the
Bourses du Travail.   It would not do to hurry decisions; the
methodical pursuit of the development of our institutions is
sufficient to realize our aim, and to avoid many disappoint-
ments and retrogressions.   It is for us, who have inherited
the thought and the science of all those who have come before us, to bring it about that so many riches and so much
welfare due to their genius should not serve to engender
misery and injustice, but should establish harmony of interests on equality of rights and on the solidarity of all human
beings.[1]

The report of the Federal Committee, prepared by Pelloutier, contained the same ideas but emphasized some other
points.   " We start out from the principle," read this re-

[1] F. Pelloutier, *op. cit.*, p. 163.

port, " that the task of the revolution is to free mankind not only from all authority (*autorité*), but also from every institution which has not for its essential purpose the development of production. Consequently, we can imagine the future society only as a voluntary and free association of producers." [1]   In this social system the syndicats and the Bourses are to play the part assigned to them in the report of the Bourse of Nimes.

The consequence of this new state, of this suppression of useless social organs, of this simplification of necessary machinery, will be that man will produce better, more and quicker; that he will be able, therefore, to devote long hours to his intellectual development, to accelerate in this way mechanical progress, to free himself more and more from painful work, and to arrange his life in greater conformity to his instinctive aspirations toward studious repose.

Pelloutier laid emphasis on the idea that this future state was being gradually prepared and was dependent upon the intellectual and moral development of the working-class; he conceived it as a gradual substitution of institutions evolved by the working-class for those institutions which characterize existing society.   He believed that the syndicalist life was the only means of stimulating the power and the initiative of the workingmen and of developing their administrative abilities.   His report, quoted above, concluded: " And this is the future in store for the working-class, if becoming conscious of its intellectual faculties, and of its dignity, it will come to draw only from within itself its notion of social duty, will detest and break every authority foreign to it and will finally conquer security and liberty." [2]

This conception of the syndicat has since become funda-

[1] F. Pelloutier, *op. cit.*, pp. 163-4.

[2] Seilhac, *Congrès Ouvriers*, p. 317.

mental with revolutionary syndicalists. Formulating it, the
Fédération des Bourses du Travail really laid the foundations of what later became revolutionary syndicalism.
The " Federation of Bourses " also made the first step in
the propaganda of anti-militarism and in outlining a policy
of opposition to the State. The latter ideas, however, were
at the same time developed in the General Confederation
of Labor and will be considered in connection with the history of that body in the next chapter.

From 1894 to 1902 the *Fédération des Bourses du Travail* was the strongest syndical organization in France.
Pelloutier claimed 250,000 members for it, but the figure
is exaggerated. There is no way, however, of finding out
the true figures.

Conscious of its comparative strength, the Federation of
Bourses at times ignored, at times dominated the General
Confederation of Labor. These two organizations were
rivals. The General Confederation of Labor had adopted
at Limoges (1895) statutes according to which the Confederation could admit not only National Federations of Syndicats, but single syndicats and single Bourses. This was
obnoxious to the Federation of Bourses. The latter wished
that the General Confederation should be composed exclusively of two federal committees; one representing the Federation of Bourses; the other representing the National
Federations of trade. Until this was accepted, the Federation of Bourses, at its Congress in Tours (1896), refused to give any financial aid to the General Confederation
in view " of the little vitality " which it displayed.

The General Confederation of Labor modified its statutes year after year, but no harmony between the two organizations could be established for some time. In 1897,
the Federation of Bourses joined the General Confederation, but left it again in 1898.

The friction was due partly to personal difficulties, partly to the differences of spirit which prevailed in the central committees of the two organizations. After 1900, however, the two organizations, though distinct, co-operated, and the question of unifying the two organizations was more and more emphasized. In 1902, at the Congress of Montpellier, this unity was realized; the Federation of Bourses entered the General Confederation of Labor, and ceased to have a separate existence.

CHAPTER IV

THE GENERAL CONFEDERATION OF LABOR FROM 1895 TO 1902

THE General Confederation of Labor has continued its existence under the same name since its foundation in 1895. Still the period from 1895 to 1902 may be considered separately for two reasons: first, during this period the organization of the Confederation under which it now functions was evolved;[1] and secondly, during this period the tendency known as revolutionary syndicalism became definite and complete. This period may be considered therefore as the formative period both from the point of view of organization and from the point of view of doctrine.

The gradual elaboration of organization and of doctrine may best be considered from year to year. The 700 syndicats which formed the General Confederation at Limoges in 1895 aimed to "establish among themselves daily relations which would permit them to formulate in common the demands studied individually; they wanted also and particularly to put an end to the disorganization which penetrated their ranks under cover of the political spirit."[2]

The Congress held the following year at Tours (1896)

---

[1] The changes in the form of organization which have been made since 1902 are in harmony with the fundamental ideas of the constitution adopted in 1902.

[2] *XI Congrès National Corporatif* (Paris, 1900), p. 35.

showed that the aim was not attained. Only 32 organizations had paid the initiation fee (two francs) as requested by the statutes adopted at Limoges. Of the 32 only four, the *Fédération des Travailleurs du Livre*,[1] the Syndicat of Railway Men, the Circle of Machinists, and the Federation of Porcelain Workers, paid their dues regularly; the rest paid irregularly or did not pay at all. The entire income for the year amounted to 740 francs.[2]

The National Council of the Confederation did not function because the number of delegates elected by the adhering organizations was insufficient to constitute the committees among which the work was to be divided. The few delegates that did attend the meetings quarreled for political and other reasons. The Federation of Bourses showed itself hostile, because the statutes adopted at Limoges admitted Bourses, single syndicats, local and regional federations.

The "Committee for the propaganda of the General Strike" could also report but little progress. The Committee had been authorized by the Congress of Nantes (1894) to collect 10 per cent of all subscriptions for strikes. The Committee, however, reported to the Congress of Tours, that the syndicats and Bourses did not live up to the decision. From December 1, 1894, to September 12, 1892, 329 francs 75 centimes was collected; for 1895–96, 401 francs 95 centimes. With such limited means but little headway could be made.[3]

The Congress of Tours tried to remedy the situation by making several changes in the statutes. Single Bourses were not to be admitted. This was a concession to the Federation of Bourses, which was invited to

---

[1] Typographical Union.   [2] Seilhac, p. 328.

[3] Seilhac, *Congrès Ouvriers*, p. 325; Ch. Franck, *op. cit.*, p. 323.

join the Confederation; single syndicats were to be admitted only if there were no national federations in their trades.   Each National Federation of trade or of industry could send three delegates to the National Council; syndicats and local federations, only one.   Each delegate to the National Council could represent two organizations only, while formerly he could represent five.   The National Council was to nominate an executive committee consisting of a secretary, assistant secretary, treasurer, assistant treasurer, and archivist.   The work of the Confederation was to be divided among seven committees.   Dues were to be paid on a graduated scale according to membership.

Besides modifying the statutes, the Congress of Tours discussed several other questions; eight-hour day, weekly rest, the general strike and the establishment of a trade organ.

The idea of the general strike, defended by Alemanists and anarchists, was indorsed by the Congress with a greater majority than at previous Congresses.   By this time, however, several modifications had taken place in the conception of the general strike.   These were emphasized by M. Guerard who defended the idea before the Congress.   Said M. Guerard:

The conquest of political power is a chimera; there are at present only three or four true socialists in the Chamber of Deputies out of 585.   Of 36,000 communes, only 150 have as yet been conquered.

The partial strikes fail because the workingmen become demoralized and succumb under the intimidation of the employers protected by the government.   The general strike will last a short while and its repression will be impossible; as to intimidation, it is still less to be feared.   The necessity of defending the factories, workshops, manufactures, stores, etc., will scatter and disperse the army. . . .

And then, in the fear that the strikes may damage the railways, the signals, the works of art, the government will be obliged to protect the 39,000 kilometers of railroad lines by drawing up the troops all along them. The 300,000 men of the active army, charged with the surveillance of 39 million meters, will be isolated from one another by 130 meters, and this can be done only on the condition of abandoning the protection of the depots, of the stations, of the factories, etc. . . . and of abandoning the employers to themselves, thus leaving the field free in the large cities to the revolted workingmen.

The principal force of the general strike consists in its power of imposing itself. A strike in one trade, in one branch of industry, must involve other branches.

The general strike can not be decreed in advance; it will burst forth suddenly: a strike of the railway men, for instance, if declared, will be the signal of the general strike. It will be the duty of militant workingmen, when this signal is given, to make their comrades in the syndicats leave their work. Those who continue to work on that day will be compelled, or forced, to quit.[1]

And M. Guerard, applauded by the audience, concluded: "The general strike will be the Revolution, peaceful or not."

However, as a concession to the opponents of the general strike, the Congress of Tours decided that the "Committee for the propaganda of the general strike" should be independent of the Confederation. It was also from now on to collect only five per cent of all strike-subscriptions.

The Congress of Tours also admonished the syndicats to abandon their political preoccupations which were held to be the cause of disorganization.

These changes helped but little. During 1896–97 the

---

[1] Seilhac, *Congrès Ouvriers*, pp. 331-2.

Confederation counted 11 federations, 1 federated union, 1 trade union, the Union of Syndicats of Paris, and three national syndicats. The Federation of Bourses declined either to join or to help the Confederation. The number of delegates to the National Council was again insufficient to constitute the committees. The income for the year, including the balance from the previous year, amounted to 1,558 francs.[1]

The Congress of Toulouse, therefore, decided to make new changes. Accepting the suggestion of the Federation of Bourses whose adherence was desired, the Confederation was to consist now of (1) the Federation of Bourses du Travail, (2) of National federations of trade and of industry, and (3) of local syndicats or of local federations of trades which were not yet organized nationally or whose national federations refused to join the Confederation. The Confederation was to be represented by the Federal Committee of the Federation of Bourses and by the National Council of the Federations of trade.

The Congress of Toulouse again declared that "the general strike was synonymous with Revolution," and decided that sub-committees for the propaganda of the general strike should be established in the *Bourses du Travail* to keep in touch with the General Committee in Paris. It discussed several other questions: trade-journal, suppression of prison-work, eight-hour day, and among these, for the first time, the questions of the boycott and of sabotage.

The report on boycott and *sabotage*[2] was prepared by two anarchists, Pouget and Delessale. The report ex-

---

[1] Ch. Franck, *op. cit.*, pp. 226-7.

[2] *Sabotage* means the obstruction in all possible ways of the regular process of production; *cf.* ch. v.

plained the origin of the boycott and of *sabotage*, and
gave instances of their application in different countries.
It referred in particular to the *Go Canny* practice of the
English workingmen whose principle the report merely
wanted to generalize and to formulate.

Up to the present time [read the report] the workingmen have
declared themselves revolutionary; but most of the time they
have remained on theoretical ground: they have labored to
extend the ideas of emancipation, they have tried to sketch a
plan of a future society from which human exploitation should
be eliminated.

But why, beside this educational work, the necessity of which
is incontestable, has nothing been tried in order to resist the
encroachments of capitalists and to render the exigencies of
employers less painful to the workingmen?

To this end the report recomended the use of the boycott and of *sabotage*, which should take place by the side
of the strike as the workingmen's means of defense and
offense.   The report shows how these methods could be
used in particular cases.   *Sabotage* particularly, sometimes applied to the quantity, sometimes to the quality,
should bring home to the employer that the workingmen
are determined to render " poor work for poor pay ".
   The report concluded:

The boycott and its indispensable complement, sabotage, furnishes us with an effective means of resistance which—while
awaiting the day when the workingmen will be sufficiently
strong to emancipate themselves completely—will permit us to
stand our ground against the exploitation of which we are the
victims.
   It is necessary that the capitalists should know it: the
workingman will respect the machine only on that day when it
shall have become for him a friend which shortens labor, in-

stead of being, as it now is, the enemy, the robber of bread, the killer of workingmen.[1]

The Congress adopted unanimously and with great enthusiasm a motion inviting the workingmen to apply the boycott and *sabotage* when strikes would not yield results.

During 1897–98 the Federation of Bourses and the Confederation were to work together, but no harmony was possible. The report presented to the Congress of Rennes (1898) is full of complaints and of accusations on both sides. Personal difficulties between the two secretaries, M. Pelloutier and M. Lagailse, who was an " Allemanist," sprang up ; besides, the National Council and the Federal Committee were animated by a different spirit. The Federal Committee evidently tried to dominate the National Council. The latter was weak. It counted only 18 organizations, and no new members were gained during 1897–98. The National Council did not function regularly; the explanation given was that as no functionaries were paid, they had but little time to devote to the business of the Confederation. The dues paid during 1897–8 amounted to 793 francs ; the whole income was 1,702 francs. The treasurer thought that this showed that the " General Confederation of Labor was in a flourishing condition."

The " Committee for the propaganda of the General Strike " admitted on the contrary that it had accomplished little. Only twenty Bourses formed sub-committes. The five per cent of strike subscriptions was not paid by the syndicats. Only 835 francs came in from this source ; together with the income from other

[1] E. Pouget, *Le Sabotage* (Paris, 1910), pp. 15-16.

sources, the receipts of the Committee totaled 1,086 francs; of this it spent 822 francs.

During 1898 the Syndicat of Railroad Workers had a conflict with the railroad companies and a railroad strike was imminent. The Secretary of the General Confederation of Labor sent out a circular to all syndical organizations of France calling their attention to the "formidable consequences for capitalism" which such a strike could have, if joined by all trades. The circular formulated eight demands, such as old-age pensions; eight-hour day, etc., which "could be realized in a few days if the working-class, conscious of its force, and of its rights, was willing to act energetically." [1]

The "Committee for the propaganda of the general strike" also took up the question. It sent out a question to all syndicats for a referendum vote. The question was: "Are you for an immediate general strike in case the railroad workingmen should declare a strike?" The report of the Committee to the Congress of Rennes complained that the syndicats voted for the general strike at conventions but changed their opinions or their disposition "when the hour for action came." [2] "It was disastrous to make such a discovery," read the report,

when it was expected that by the strike of our comrades of the railroads, many other trades would be compelled by the force of events to quit work, and that this would have been the starting-point of the general strike, and possibly of that economic revolution which alone can solve the great problems which confront the entire world. [3]

[1] X Congrès National Corporatif (IV de la C. G. T.), Rennes, 1898, p. 77.

[2] X Congès National Corporatif (Rennes, 1898), p. 334.

[3] Ibid., p. 334.

The Syndicat of the Railroad Workingmen voted for a strike. But the government intercepted the strike order of the National Committee of the Syndicat, and the strike did not take place.

The Congress of Rennes made new changes in the statutes of the Confederation. The Federation of Bourses was to leave the Confederation. The latter was to be composed only of national federations of trade and of national syndicats and to be represented by the National Council. The "Committee of the general strike" was to be part of the Confederation, but was to be autonomous and was to live on its own resources.

The Congress discussed a number of questions : Alcoholism, suppression of employment bureaus, election of inspectors of industry, etc. Most reports on the various questions adopted by the Congress assert that the workingmen must solicit the co-operation of their representatives in the legislative bodies of the country in order to obtain any reforms. But one report was presented which emphasized the opposite idea of "direct action".

This report was presented by the "Committee on the Label, the Boycott, and *Sabotage*." The reporter on the boycott and *sabotage*—M. Pouget—noted the little progress that had been accomplished in the application of these two methods since 1897, but again affirmed their validity and recommended them to the workingman ; the report affirmed that the menace, only, of sabotage is often sufficient to produce results. "The Congress," said the report,

cannot enter into the details of these tactics; such things depend upon the initiative and the temperament of each and are subordinate to the diversity of industries. We can only lay down the theory and express the wish that the boycott and the *sabotage* should enter into the arsenal of weapons which the workingmen use in their struggle against capitalists on the same plane as the strike, and that, more and more, the direction of the social movement should be towards the direct action of individuals and towards a greater consciousness of their personal powers.[1]

The Congress of Paris (1900) again recorded but little progress. In the interval since Rennes (1898–1900) only a few new federations joined the General Confederation. The others, whose adherence was solicited, refused or even were not " polite enough " to make a reply. The adhering organizations paid irregularly; the decisions of the Congresses were not executed. The Committees still did not function because the number of delegates to the National Council was small. The total income for both years amounted to 3,678 francs, of which 1,488 were dues paid.

The "Committee for the propaganda of the general strike" had collected during this period (1898–1900) 4,262 francs. Of this 3,172 francs were the five per cent of the strike subscriptions. It may also be interesting to note that the organizations which contributed most to this sum were: Union of Syndicats of Seine, 901 francs; the Union of Machinists of Seine, 727 francs; the Federation of Moulders, 536 francs; the Federation of Metallurgy, 457 francs. The Committee published thirteen numbers of a journal, "The General Strike," and a brochure on the general strike.

The general strike was again the subject of a long discussion at the Congress of Paris. But the discussion was given a new turn. The question now was: "The general strike, its organization, its eventuality, its consequences." And the ideas that prevailed revealed some further modifications in the conception.

[1] X Congrès National Corporatif (Rennes, 1898), p. 302.

The question was given this turn because certain syndicats thought that the principle of the general strike had been sufficiently affirmed and that it was time to treat the subject practically. As the discussion showed, the majority of the delegates thought that the general strike could take place at any moment and that in order to be successful, it did not presuppose a majority of organized workingmen, nor big sums of money. A daring revolutionary minority conscious of its aim could carry away with it the majority of workingmen and accomplish the act of appropriating the means of production for society as a whole. Some even thought that in order that the general strike should be prompt and lead to the aim in view it was best to have no money at all; everyone would then take what he needed wherever he found it, and the result would be the completest possible emancipation."[1] As one of the delegates expressed it: "Count exclusively upon the enthusiasm (*entrainement*) of the working-class."[2]

This conception of the general strike attributed to the syndicat a revolutionary rôle, as the syndicat was to take possession of the means of production in the name of society as a whole. It did not exclude however the parallel action of political parties. The latter could profit by the general strike and seize the political power of the State to co-operate in the transformation of society. But the syndicats were not to count upon this possibility; on the contrary it was their task to make the general strike absolutely independent of all political parties, to perform the principal part in the economic revolution and to leave to the new government, if one

---

[1] *XI Congrès National Corporatif* (Paris, 1900), p. 198.

[2] *Ibid.*, p. 113.

arose, no other function but that of sanctioning the economic change accomplished by the syndicats.

This emphasis upon the revolutionary and preponderant part to be played by the syndicats went together with a mistrust and defiance of political parties. "All politicians are betrayers,"[1] exclaimed one delegate. "In politics one has always to deal with intrigues," said another, and the same sentiment pervaded the other speeches. Though not refusing to make use of all methods, "for the disorganization of capitalism," all delegates emphasized the necessity for the workingmen to rely mainly upon themselves and upon their syndical organizations.

The majority of delegates recognized also that the general strike must necessarily have a violent character. Though a few still thought of the general strike as of a "peaceful revolution," a "strike of folded arms," the majority rejected this conception as childish and foresaw the inevitable collision to which the general strike would lead.

All these ideas were briefly summarized in the conclusions of the Committee appointed by the Congress to report on the question. This Commission recommended leaving the "Committee for the propaganda of the general strike" as free as possible in its action. The Congress merely determined the syndicats which were to elect the members of the Committee. The latter was now to obtain regular monthly dues for the continuation of its work.

The revolutionary spirit which manifested itself in the conception of the general strike expressed itself also in the resolution of the Congress on the army. This resolution demanded the suppression of permanent armies, and in-

[1] *XI Congrès National Corporatif* (Paris, 1900), p. 110.

vited the syndicats to establish relations with the work-ingmen in military service, to invite them to social gatherings and to assist them financially (to establish the so-called *Sou du Soldat*).

The same spirit characterized the report of the Committee which formulated the ideas of the Congress on the " practical means of realizing the international harmony of the workingmen." " Capital," read the report, " in its various forms is international," and it is necessary that labor should also be organized internationally.. The slight differences in conditions of life varying from country to country are not important. " The predominating fact everywhere, in all countries, is the division of society into two categories ; the producer and the non-producer, the wage-earner and the employer." The report went on to say that the idea of "fatherland" (*patrie*) is a means of protecting the strong against the weak, " an emblem of speculation, of exploitation," "a synonym of property," " a fiction for the workingmen who posesses nothing." [1] The practical conclusion of the Committee was to bring together the wage-earners of all countries in an international organization which should be represented by an international secretariat.

During 1900-1 the Confederation displayed a little more activity than before. The National Council employed a permanent employee to attend to the business of the Confederation, at first for two, then for four hours a day at a remuneration of 50 and then 100 francs a month. In December, 1900, the Confederation began also to publish its own weekly, *La Voix du Peuple*. Since 1896 the question of a trade-journal had been on the order of the day. It was discussed at every Congress and various

[1] *XI Congrès National Corporatif* (Paris, 1900), p. 205.

plans were recommended in order to obtain the financial means for a daily. The Congress of Paris, in view of the financial impossibility of starting a daily and recognizing that "it was more than ever necessary to create a revolutionary syndicalist organ," decided to publish a weekly. One of the Committees of the National Council was to attend to it.

The *Voix du Peuple*, however, was not in a satisfactory condition at the time of the Congress of Lyons (1901). Pouget, the editor of the paper and the secretary of the Committee of the *Voix du Peuple*, complained that the *Voix du Peuple*, "suffered from the apathy and the negligence of the comrades." Only 260 syndicats subscribed for the paper (out of 2,700 syndicats then in existence). In Paris only 600 copies were sold weekly. The finances showed a deficit for the year of over 6,000 francs. The number of copies printed fell from 12,000–14,000 during the first months to 800 during the later months.

The secretary of the Confederation, M. Guerard, also complained that the "Confederation was anaemic for lack of means." The twenty organizations—federations and syndicats—which adhered to the Confederation during 1900–1901 paid in 1,478 francs. The total income was 4,125 francs. With such limited means the Confederation could do nothing. The Congress of Lyons (1901) —where all these reports were read—was provided for by a subvention from the municipality of Lyons which appropriated 7,000 francs for the purpose.

The Congress of Lyons, nevertheless, showed that the Confederation was beginning to feel a little more confidence in its future. The Congress decided that henceforth only syndicats adhering to the Confederation should take part in its Congresses. Previous to that all syndicats were invited to send a delegate or their mandate to the Congresses of the Confederation. The Congresses, therefore, neither revealed the strength of the Confederation, nor had a binding character, and were significant merely as revealing the state of mind of a large part of the organized workingmen of the time. The decision of the Congress of Lyons was to do away with this condition and to give the Congresses of the Confederation a more coherent and binding character.

Another decision taken by the Congress of Lyons was to admit local and regional federations of syndicats. This was directed against the Federation of Bourses. Though more friendly since 1900, the relations between the two organizations still gave trouble. The question of unity, however, was urged by many workingmen, and the Congress decided to call a special Congress for 1902 to solve this problem.

The Congress of Lyons revealed the further progress of revolutionary ideas among the delegates. There were 226 delegates; these represented 26 Bourses and 8 local federations, comprising 1,035 syndicats with 245,000 members;[1] eight regional federations composed of 264 syndicats with 36,000 members; 8 federations of trade or industry counting 507 syndicats with 196,000 members; 492 syndicats with 60,000 workingmen were represented directly. The exact number of syndicats and of work-

---

[1] The growth of syndicats in France since 1895 is shown in the following table:

Year	Syndicats	Members
1895	2,163	419,781
1896	2,243	422,777
1898	2,324	437,793
1899	2,361	419,761
1900	2,685	492,647
1901	3,287	588,832

ingmen represented cannot be obtained from these figures, because one syndicat could be represented several
times in a local federation, in a Bourse, and in the federation of trade.   The delegates, however, came from
different parts of the country and were numerous enough
to show that the ideas they expressed were accepted by
a considerable number of French workingmen.

Of the questions discussed at Lyons three had a particular significance as showing the revolutionary tendency which the Confederation was taking.   These were
the questions of the general strike, of labor-laws, and of
the relations to the political parties.

The "Committee for the propaganda of the General
Strike" reported more activity for the year 1900–1 and
greater success in its work.   The Committee published
a brochure on the General Strike of which 50,000 copies
were distributed.   It collected over 1,500 francs in
monthly dues, and its total income amounted to 2,447
francs.   It was in touch with a number of sub-committees in the different *Bourses du Travail*, arranged a
number of meetings on various occasions, and lent its
support to some strikes.   The Committee affirmed that
the idea of the general strike had spread widely during
the year and attributed this fact to the big strikes which
had taken place in France after the International Exhibition of 1900 and which had thrown the workingmen
into a state of agitation.

At the time the Congress of Lyons was being held,
the miners were threatening to strike, if their demands
were not granted by the companies.   The delegate of
the miners was at the Congress, and the discussion that
took place under these conditions was very characteristic.

The Committee on the general strike which consisted
of fifteen members reported:

The idea of the general strike is sufficiently understood to-day.
In repeatedly putting off the date of its coming, we risk discrediting it forever by enervating the revolutionary energies.

What better occasion to realize it!

The miners will give the signal on the first of November; the working-class—in case of a revolution—counts upon this movement which must bring them their economic liberation.

And the report of the Committee went on to point out the conditions which in its opinion indicated "that the moment had come to try the general strike (*faire la Grève générale*) with strong chances of success."[1]

The delegate from the miners said: "If you wish to join us, we will be able not only to strike, but to bring about the revolution; if we were made sure of the co-operation of all trades, even if it were necessary to wait for it two, three, or even six months, we are ready to grant you this concession."[2]

The following motion was then adopted:

The Congress declares that the General Strike cannot be the means merely of obtaining amelioration for any category of workingmen.

Its aim can be only the complete emancipation of the proletariat through the violent expropriation of the capitalist class.

The Congress, in view of the situation, declares that the movement which may take place in favor of the miners, the importance or character of which nobody can foresee and which may go to the point of a general emancipation, will be in any case a movement of solidarity which will not impair in the least the revolutionary principle of the general strike of all workingmen.[3]

The delegate of the Typographical Union (*La Fédéra-*

[1] *XII Congrès National Corporatif* (Lyons, 1901), p. 170.
[2] *Ibid.*, pp. 177-8.   [3] *Ibid.*, p. 179.

tion du Livre) combated the idea of the general strike and argued that it was impossible in view of the small number of organized workingmen. But his argument had no effect on the Congress. It was rejected as of no importance because the minority of organized working-men could carry away with it the majority.

The question of labor laws was the subject of an animated discussion at the Congress because of its importance. The answer given to this question was to determine the attitude of the General Confederation to legislative reforms and to the State in general.

The question was a very practical one. The government of Waldeck-Rousseau (22 June, 1899–6 June, 1902), in which the socialist, Millerand, was Minister of Commerce and Industry, outlined a number of labor laws which touched upon the most vital questions of the labor movement. The most important of these law-projects were on strikes and arbitration, on the composition of the superior Council of Labor, on the institution of Councils of Labor, and on the modification of the law of 1884.

The policy of the government in planning these laws was clear and expressly stated. It was the continuation and accentuation of the policy which had guided M. Waldeck-Rousseau in 1884 when he was Minister of the Interior in the Cabinet of Jules Ferry, and which had then found partial expression in the ministerial circular on the application of the new law on syndicats.

This "Circular," sent out to the Prefects August 25, 1884, pointed out to the Prefects that it was the duty of the State not merely to watch over the strict observation of the law, but "to favor the spirit of association" among the workingmen and "to stimulate" the latter to make use of the new right. In the conception of the government the syndicats were to be "less a weapon of struggle" than "an instrument of material, moral and intellectual progress." It was "the wish of the Government and of the Chambers to see the propagation, in the largest possible measure, of the trade associations and of the institutions which they were destined to engender" (such as old-age pension funds, mutual credit banks, libraries, co-operative societies, etc.) and the government expected the Prefects "to lend active assistance" in the organization of syndicats and in the creation of syndical institutions.[1]

The aim of Waldeck-Rousseau was to bring about the "alliance of the bourgeoise and of the working-class"[2] which Gambetta and other republican statesmen had untiringly preached as the only condition of maintaining the Republic. In the period 1899–1902 this policy seemed still more indispensable. It was the time when the agitation caused by the Dreyfus affair assumed the character of a struggle between the republican and anti-republican forces of France. Republicans, Radicals, Socialists, and Anarchists were fighting hand in hand against Monarchists, Nationalists, Anti-Semites and Clericals. The cabinet of Waldeck-Rousseau constituted itself a "Cabinet of Republican Defense" and it sought to attain its end by securing the support of all republican elements of the country. This was the cause which prompted Waldeck-Rousseau to invite a socialist, Millerand, to enter his cabinet and to accentuate his policy of attaching the working-class to the Republic by a series of protective labor laws.

[1] See the "Circulaire" in G. Severac, *Guide Pratique des Syndicats Professionnels* (Paris, 1908), pp. 125-136.

[2] G. Hanoteaux, *Modern France* (tr. by J. C. Tarver, New York, 1903-09), vol. ii, p. 181.

The policy of the Government was clearly expressed by Millerand in the Chamber of Deputies on November 23, 1899. "It has appeared to me," said he, "that the best means for bringing back the working masses to the Republic, is to show them not by words, but by facts, that the republican government is above everything else the government of the small and of the weak."[1]

The facts by which M. Millerand undertook to show this were a number of decrees by which the government tried to enforce a stricter observation of labor-laws already in existence and a series of new law-projects for the future protection of labor, such as the bill on a ten-hour day, which became law on March 30, 1900. As M. Millerand expressed it, this law was "a measure of moralization, of solidarity, and of social pacification."

Social pacification was the supreme aim of M. Millerand and of the government. M. Millerand hoped to attain this by calling workingmen to participation in the legislative activities of the Republic, by accustoming them to peaceable discussions with employers, and by regulating the more violent forms of the economic struggle.

A decree from September 1, 1899, modified the constitution of the Superior Council of Labor, in existence since 1891, so that it should henceforth consist of 22 elected workingmen, 22 elected employers and 22 members appointed by the Minister from among the deputies of the Chamber, the senators and other persons representing "general interests." The Superior Council of Labor was "an instrument of study, of information and of consultation" in matters of labor legislation. It studied law-projects affecting the conditions of labor,

[1] A. Lavy, *L'Oeuvre de Millerand* (Paris, 1902), p. 2.

made its own suggestions to the government, but had no legislative powers.

The decree of M. Millerand was particularly significant in one respect: it called upon the workingmen organized in the syndicats to elect fifteen members of the Superior Council of Labor. M. Millerand pointed out the significance of this measure in a speech delivered on June 5, 1900. Said he:

The workingmen are henceforth warned, that in order to participate through delegates sprung from their own ranks in the elaboration of economic reforms which concern them most, it is necessary and sufficient that they enter the ranks of that great army of which the syndicats are the battalions. How can they refuse to do this? By inducing them to do so we believe that we are defending their legitimate interests at the same time that we are serving the cause of social peace in this country.[1]

The "Councils of Labor" were organized by two decrees from September 17, 1900, and from January 2, 1901. Composed of an equal number of workingmen and of employers, these Councils had for their principal mission to enlighten the government, as well as workingmen and employers, on the actual and necessary conditions of labor, to facilitate thereby industrial harmony and general agreement between the interested parties, to furnish in cases of collective conflicts competent mediators, and to inform the public authorities on the effects produced by labor legislation.[1]

M. Millerand emphasized that the Councils of Labor were to bring workingmen and employers together for the discussion of "their general interests" and that this

---

[1] A. Lavy, *op. cit.*, p. 66. [2] *Ibid.*, p. 79.

new institution would be one more motive for the utilization of the law of 1884 on syndicats. "To encourage by all means the formation of these trade-associations, so useful for the progress of social peace," wrote the Minister in his decree, "is a task which a republican government cannot neglect."[1]

To enlarge the possible operations of the syndicats, the government also introduced a bill into the Chamber (November 14, 1899) which contained several modifications of the law of 1884. This bill proposed to extend the commercial capacities of the syndicat and to grant the syndicat the rights of a juridical person.

To complete the series of measures which were to impart a peaceful character to the syndical movement, M. Millerand introduced into the chamber a bill (November 15, 1900) on the regulation of strikes and on arbitration. This law-project proposed a complicated mechanism for the settlement of economic conflicts. It hinged on the principle that strikes should be decided by secret ballot and by a majority vote renewed at brief intervals by all workingmen concerned; permanent arbitration boards in the industrial establishments were part of the mechanism.[2]

Toward this series of labor laws the Congress of Lyons was to define its attitude. The principle of the Superior Council of Labor was accepted by a majority of 258 against 205 votes (5 blank); the project on the regulation of strikes and on arbitration was rejected by a unanimous vote minus five; the Councils of Labor proposition was rejected by a majority of 279 against 175 (18 blank).

---

[1] A. Lavy, *op. cit.*, p. 80.

[2] Only the most important measures of M. Millerand are mentioned; they do not by any means exhaust his legislative activities during this period.

The discussion on the labor laws brought out the fact that the idea of " direct action " had undergone further modifications as a result of the policy of the government. M. Waldeck-Rousseau was denounced by the speakers as "a clever defender of the interests of the bourgeoisie" who wished merely to stop the offensive movement of the workingmen ".[1] The legislative measures of the " pseudo-socialist minister ",[2] Millerand, were interpreted as schemes for restraining the revolutionary action of the syndicats. The workingmen were warned that, if they accepted the laws, they would " reinforce a power which they wanted to destroy".[4] They were reminded that the main function of the syndicat was to organize the workmen for their final emancipation which presupposes the "abolition of the wage-system " and that all " so-called labor laws " would only retard the hour of final liberation.

The revolutionary elements of the Congress did not deny, however, the possibility or the desirability of reforms. They insisted only upon particular methods of obtaining reforms and upon a particular kind of reforms. They rejected all peaceful discussion with employers because the interests of employers and of workingmen were held to be distinct and antagonistic. They did not want an "economic parliamentarism "[5] which would necessarily take the sting out of the workingmen's weapons and deprive the syndicats of their force. They wanted such reforms only as should "undermine the foundations"[6] of existing society and which should advance the movement for " integral emanci-

---

[1] *XII Congrès National Corporatif* (VI de la C. G. T.), Lyons, 1901, p. 110.

[2] *Ibid.*, p. 114.　　　　　[3] *Ibid.*, p. 210.

[4] *Ibid.*, p. 112.　　　　　[5] *Ibid.*, p. 218.

[6] *Ibid.*, p. 110.

pation " by strengthening the forces and the organization of the workingmen.

Such reforms could be obtained only independently of all parliamentarism ",[1] by the workingmen organized in their syndicats displaying all their initiative, manifesting all their energies, relying only upon themselves and not upon intermediaries. Only in this way would the syndicats wrest " piece by piece from capitalistic society reforms the application of which would finally give the exploited class the force which is indispensable in order to bring about the social revolution ". [2]

These ideas showed the further application which the principle of " direct action " was given by the revolutionary elements in the syndicats. The syndicats were not only to carry on their struggle " directly" against employers by strikes, boycotts and *sabotage*, but also against the State, and not only against the State appearing as the " enemy of labor", but also against the State wishing to become the protector and benefactor of the workingmen. This hostility to the State and to its reform-legislation marked a further accentuation of the ideas of revolutionary syndicalism.

The Congress of Lyons took, also, a decided stand on the relations of the syndicats to political action. Under " political action" of course the action of the Socialist parties was meant. After the foundation of the General Confederation of Labor certain important changes had taken place in the socialist movement of France which could not but have their effect upon the syndicats.

In 1893 the socialist parties had their first big success in the general elections. They obtained about 600,000

[1] *XI Congrès National Corporatif*, p. 114.

[2] *Ibid.*, p. 119.

votes[1] and elected over 50 deputies. The socialist deputies in the Chamber constituted a Parliamentary Group —*Union Socialiste*—which acted in common. This strengthened the tendency toward union which had already manifested itself, during the elections, when the Socialists had entered into unions among themselves.

The unity in action was further made possible by a unity in views which was becoming more and more manifest. After 1892, when the Guesdists obtained a large number of votes in the municipal elections and gained a number of municipalities, their ideas on some of the most important points of their program began to change. In 1894, at their Congress of Nantes, the Guesdists elaborated a detailed program of reforms designed to win the votes of the agricultural population. This program made no mention of the collective appropriation of the soil; on the contrary, it stated that, "in the agricultural domain, the means of production, which is the soil, is in many places still in the possession of the producers themselves as individual property" and that "if this state of conditions, characterized by peasant proprietorship, must inevitably disappear, socialism must not precipitate its disappearance."[2] With similar promises of reform the Guesdists addressed other classes of the population: artisans, small merchants and the lower strata of the middle classes.

Formerly ardent revolutionists, they now began to emphasize the legal aspect of their activity and the emancipating influence of universal suffrage. Jules Guesde himself in his speeches in the Chamber of Dep-

---

[1] A. Hamon, *Le Socialisme et le Congrès de Londres* (Paris, 1897), p. 11.

[2] L. Blum, *Congrès Ouvriers et Socialistes*, p. 146.

uties on various occasions expressed his belief that universal suffrage was the instrument with which all questions might be peacefully solved,[1] and that nothing but legal weapons would throw the Republic into the hands of the socialist army. G. Deville, then one of the principal theorists of the party, affirmed in 1896 that the only actual task of the party was to increase the number of socialist electors and representatives.[2] With the affirmation of the emancipating significance of universal suffrage the importance of parliamentary action was more and more emphasized.

Thus the "revolutionary" socialists were approaching the reformist elements composed of Broussists and of Independents. In 1896 this *rapprochement* was manifested at the banquet of Saint Mandé arranged on the occasion of the success obtained by the socialists during the municipal elections of that year. All socialist parties took part in it and Millerand delivered a speech in which he outlined the common points of the socialist program. This program emphasized the peaceful and evolutionary character of socialism: "We address ourselves only to universal suffrage," said Millerand, . . . "In order to begin the socialization of the means of production, it is necessary and sufficient for the Socialist party to pursue with the help of universal suffrage the conquest of the political powers."[3] Guesde, present at the banquet, approved and "applauded" the definition of Socialism given by Millerand.

The Dreyfus affair brought the socialists for some

---

[1] *Chambre des Deputés, Débats Parlémentaires;* July 11, 1895; November 22, 1895.

[2] Deville, *Principes Socialistes.*

[3] A. Millerand, *Le Socialisme Réformiste Français* (Paris, 1903), pp. 31-32.

time into still closer contact. A "Committee of Harmony" (*Comité d'Entente*) was formed in which all the
socialist organizations were represented. The demand
for unity was expressed in the socialist periodical press,
and J. Jaures outlined a plan according to which the old
separate and rival factions were to disappear in one unified party.[1] The belief in the possibility of such a unified
party was general.

The entrance of Millerand into the Ministry of Waldeck-Rousseau was a sudden shock which again disrupted the elements tending toward union. The Guesdists, Blanquists and a few other groups denounced the
act of Millerand as a violation of the principles of class
and class-struggle—the fundamental principles of Socialism. The Independents, Broussists and similar elements,
on the contrary, insisted upon the necessity of taking
part in the general life of the country and of assuming
responsibilities when they are inevitable. At two general Congresses of all socialist organizations held in
Paris (December, 1899, and September, 1900) this question was discussed. The Congresses ended with a quar-
rel among the various socialist organizations which led
to complete rupture at the following Congress in Lyons
in May, 1901. The Guesdists, Blanquists and several
regional federations formed the *Parti Socialiste de
France;* the Independents, Broussists, and Allemanists
formed the *Parti Socialiste Francais*, which supported
Millerand and the cabinet of Waldeck-Rousseau. Within
each new grouping, however, the old organizations remained intact.

The "case Millerand" raised such violent polemics,
such bitter mutual accusations among the Socialists that

[1] *Le Mouvement Socialiste*, Jan., 1899.

many members of the party felt disgusted. Even the French socialist movement, so rich in inner divisions and dissensions, had never before experienced such a critical condition.

In view of this situation the organized workingmen were anxious now more than ever to keep politics out of the syndicats. The resolution adopted unanimously by the Congress of Lyons insisted upon the fact that the introduction of politics into the syndicats would cause division in the syndicalist ranks, and therefore invited the syndicats and the federations to remain independent of all political parties, "leaving to individuals the undeniable right to devote themselves to that kind of struggle which they prefer in the political field." The syndicat as an organization, however, should remain neutral; otherwise it would be "false to its true rôle which consists in grouping all the exploited without distinction of race, nationality, philosophical or religious opinions, and political views."[1]

The reaction of socialist workingmen, however, to the situation created by the "case Millerand" was of a more complicated character. While the entrance of a socialist minister into the government aroused hopes and expectations in the minds of many, to others it seemed the beginning of the end of socialism. Habitually regarding socialism as a class-movement, imbued with the ideas of class and class-struggle, they were shocked and grieved at the "collaboration of classes" which Millerand practised in the government and the Socialists in Parliament.

To these socialist workingmen the danger seemed the greater because it presented itself as a crowning act of a policy that had been pursued for some time by all the

[1] *XII Congrès Corporatif* (Lyons, 1901), p. 151.

socialists.   As we have seen, even the revolutionary
Guesdists had become more and more moderate.   They
had co-operated in Parliament with the republican parties
and had concluded alliances during elections with "bourgeois" parties.   At the general Congress of socialists in
Paris in 1899, M. Briand in a clever and somewhat biting
speech pointed out to the revolutionary socialists that
their policy had made the "case Millerand" possible.
"It seems," said Briand, "that great astonishment has
been aroused in our comrades of the *Parti Ouvrier*
(Guesdists) by the entrance of our comrade Millerand
into a bourgeois government.   But, citizens of the *Parti
Ouvrier*, what has taken place is the very consequence
of the policy which by successive concessions you have
forced upon the entire socialist party."[1]   And Briand
pointed out these "successive concessions" which deprived the Guesdists of their revolutionary character.
To quote M. Briand again:

Yes, you become interested in these [electoral] struggles which
gave immediate results, and little by little our militant comrades also became interested in them, took a liking for them
to such a degree that they soon came to believe that in order
to triumph definitely over the capitalist society nothing was
necessary but to storm the ballot-boxes.   Thus within recent
years the country could gain the impression that the socialist
party was no longer a revolutionary party.[2]

This impression many socialist workingmen had, and
the "case Millerand" strengthened it in them.   But
preservation of the revolutionary character of socialism
was for them a necessity, equivalent to maintaining their
belief in the coming of socialism at all.   These working-

---

[1] *Congrès Général des Organisations Socialistes* (Paris, 1899), p. 152.
[2] *Ibid.*, p. 155.

men of all socialist parties, Allemanists, Blanquists, and even Guesdists, therefore, now threw themselves with greater energy into the syndicalist movement which seemed to them the only refuge for the revolutionary spirit. There they met the Communist-Anarchists who had been taking an active part in the syndicalist movement for some time. The Communist-Anarchists before 1895 had generally shown little sympathy for the syndicats where the workingmen, they said, were either engaged in politics or trying to obtain paltry reforms. But tired of carrying on a merely verbal propaganda and spurred on by Pelloutier,[1] they began to change their attitude after 1895, and after 1899 became influential in many syndicalist organizations. Their criticism of electoral action, their denunciation of political intriguing, now under the conditions created by the "case Millerand," fell on prepared ground and yielded fruit. A decided anti-political tendency gained strength in the syndicats.

This tendency was further strengthened by the economic events of the period. During these years, particularly after the Exhibition of Paris, a series of big strikes took place in various parts of France, among the miners in the north, the dockers in the ports of the south, in the Creusot works, etc. These strikes were partly the result of the large expectations aroused in the workingmen by the entrance of a socialist minister into the government. But the government sent troops against some of the strikers and in two or three cases blood was shed. The agitation aroused by the bloodshed was great and intensified the defiance toward

---

[1] To understand the change in the attitude of the anarchists towards the syndicats, the disillusioning effect of their terroristic campaign from 1890 to 1894, during which the exploits of Ravachole, Henri, Casiers, and others took place, must also be considered.

Millerand and toward the political parties in general. On the other hand, some of the strikes became more or less general in character and were won by the energetic action of the strikers. This strengthened the conviction in the efficacy of economic action and in the possibility of the general strike.

Under the combined influence of all these conditions, the socialist and anarchist workingmen, during this period, began to ascribe to the syndicats a decided preponderance in all respects, and they actively engaged in making their revolutionary ideas predominant in the syndical organizations. The resolutions and discussions at the Congress of Lyons revealed this state of mind and the progress attained. The revolutionary elements of the syndicats had by this time become conscious of themselves, and in opposition to the program of the political socialists, they advanced the idea of the General Confederation of Labor as a distinctly unifying conception which in the future was to play a great social rôle. "The General Confederation of Labor uniting all the workingmen's syndical forces," said the Secretary, Guérard, in his report to the Congress of Lyons, "is destined to become the revolutionary instrument capable of transforming society."[1] In greeting the delegates at the opening of the Congress, Bourchet addressed them as "the representatives of the great party of Labor" (*grand parti du travail*).[2] The same term was used by other delegates,[3] and in the summing-up of the work of the Congress, the emphasis was laid upon the demarcation between the syndicalists and the politicians which the Congress had clearly shown.

Thus, with the Congress of Lyons the General Con-

[1] *XI Congrès Corporatif*, (Lyons, 1901), p. 29.
[2] *Ibid.*, p. 14.   [3] *Ibid.*, p. 69.

federation of Labor may be said to have entered definitely upon the revolutionary path. The main ideas of
revolutionary syndicalism were clearly formulated and
consciously accepted. The main functionaries elected
after the Congress were revolutionists, viz., the secretary
Griffuelhes and the assistant secretary and editor of the
Voix du Peuple Pouget.

The Congress of Montpellier held next year (1902)
showed constant accentuation of the revolutionary tendencies. The Congress of Montpellier was almost entirely occupied with the elaboration of a new constitution
which would unite the General Confederation and the
Federation of Bourses. Statutes acceptable to both
organizations were adopted to go into force on January
1, 1903.

At the Congress of Montpellier the report of the Secretary Griffuelhes claimed that during the year the Confederation had made progress. But this progress was
very slight. The real growth of the Confederation began after its fusion with the Federation of Bourses.
Since then also dates the more active participation of
the Confederation in the political and social life of the
country. But before taking up the history of the General Confederation since 1902, it seems advisable to sum
up the main ideas of revolutionary syndicalism in a more
systematic way.

CHAPTER V

THE DOCTRINE OF REVOLUTIONARY SYNDICALISM

WHEN the General Confederation of Labor adopted its new constitution in 1902, the main ideas of revolutionary syndicalism had already been clearly formulated. Since then, however, a considerable amount of literature has appeared on the subject, either clarifying or further developing various points of the doctrine. This literature consists mainly of numerous articles in the periodical press and of pamphlets and is, accordingly, of an unsystematic character. The attempt is made in this chapter to sum up in a systematic way the leading ideas of revolutionary syndicalism common to all who call themselves revolutionary syndicalists. Consideration of individual ideas and of contributions of particular writers will be left to a following chapter.

The fundamental idea of revolutionary syndicalism is the idea of class-struggle. Society is divided into two classes, the class of employers who possess the instruments of production and the class of workingmen who own nothing but their labor-power and who live by selling it.

Between the two classes an incessant struggle is going on. This struggle is a fact, not a theory in need of proof. It is a fact manifested every day in the relations between employers and wage-earners, a fact inherent in the economic organization of existing society.

The class-struggle is not a fact to be deplored; on the contrary, it should be hailed as the creative force in so-

ciety, as the force which is working for the emancipation
of the working-class. It is the class-struggle which is
consolidating the workingmen into a compact unity opposed to the exploitation and domination of employers.
It is the class-struggle which is evolving new ideas of
right (*droit*) in opposition to the existing law. It is
the class-struggle which is developing the self-conscious-
ness, the will-power and the moral character of the
workingmen and is creating forms of organization proper
to them. In a word, it is the class-struggle which is
forging the material and moral means of emancipation
for the workingmen and putting these weapons into
their hands.

The task of the syndicalists is to organize the more or
less vague class-feeling of the workingmen and to raise
it to the clear consciousness of class-interests and of
class-ideals. This aim can be attained only by organizing the workingmen into syndicats. The syndicat is an
association of workingmen of the same or of similar
trades, and is held together by bonds of common interest. In this is its strength. Of all human groupings it
is the most fundamental and the most permanent, because men in society are interested above everything else
in the satisfaction of their economic needs.

The strength, permanence, and class-character of economic groups are made conspicuous by comparison with
forms of grouping based on other principles. Political
parties, groups of idealists, or communities professing a
common creed, are associations which cannot but be
weak and transient in view of their heterogeneous composition and of the accidental character of their bond of
union. Political bodies, for instance, are made up of
men of various interests grouped only by community of
ideas. This is true even of the Socialist party which

consists of manufacturers, financiers, doctors, and lawyers, as well as of workingmen. Even the Socialist party cannot, therefore, make prominent the class-division of society, and tends to merge all classes into one conglomeration which is unstable and incapable of persistent collective action. Only in groupings of real and fundamental interests such as the syndicats, are men of the same conditions brought together for purposes inextricably bound up with life.

The syndicat groups men of one and the same trade in their capacity of workingmen only, regardless of any other qualifications. The workingmen entering a syndicat may be Catholics or Protestants, Republicans, Socialists, or Monarchists, they may be of any color, race or nationality; in their capacity of workingmen they are all equally welcome and legitimate members of the syndicat. A workingman enrolling in a syndicat is not entering a party, not subscribing to a platform, nor accepting a creed. He is simply entering into a relation which is forced upon him by his very position in society, and is grouping himself with his fellowmen in such a way as to derive more strength for himself in the struggle for existence, contributing at the same time to the strength of his fellowmen.

These conditions make the syndicat peculiarly fit to serve the interests of the workingmen. The syndicat is a sphere of influence which by the volume of its suggestion and by the constancy and intensity of its action shapes the feelings and ideas of the workingmen after a certain pattern. In the syndicat the workingmen forget the things which divide them and are intent upon that which unites them. In the syndicat the workingmen meet to consider common interests, to discuss their identical situation, to plan together for defense and aggression, and in all ways are made to feel their group-solidarity and their antagonism to the class of employers.

In view of this the syndicats should prefer industrial unionism to craft unionism. The separation of working-men into trades is apt to develop in them a corporate spirit which is not in harmony with the class-idea. The industrial union, on the contrary, widens the mental horizon of the workingman and his.range of solidarity with his fellow workers and thus serves better to strengthen his class-consciousness.

The syndicat is the instrument with which the working-men can enter into a "direct" struggle with employ-ers. "Direct action" is what the syndicalists most insist upon, as the only means of educating the workingmen and of preparing them for the final act of emancipation. "Direct action" is action by the workingmen themselves without the help of intermediaries; it is not necessarily violent action, though it may assume violent forms; it is the manifestation of the consciousness and of the will of the workingmen themselves, without the intervention of an external agent: it consists in pressure exerted di-rectly by those interested for the sake of obtaining the ends in view.

"Direct action" may assume various forms, but the principal ones in the struggle against employers are: the strike, the boycott, the label, and *sabotage,*

The strike, in the view of the syndicalists, is the mani-festation of the class-struggle *par excellence*. The strike brings the workingmen face to face with the employers in a clash of interests. A strike clears up, as if by a flash of lightning, the deep antagonism which exists between those who employ and those who work for employers. It further deepens the chasm between them, consolida-ting the employers on the one hand, and the workingmen

on the other, over against one another. It is a revolutionary fact of great value

All strikes, partial, general in a locality, or general in
some one trade, have this revolutionary influence, particularly when they are conducted in a certain way. If
the workingmen rely only on their treasury, the strike
degenerates into a mere contest between two money
bags—that of the employer and that of the syndicat—
and loses much of its value. Still more are the syndicalists opposed to methods of conciliation and arbitration. The idea of the revolutionary syndicalists is
that a strike should be won by *Sturm und Drang*, by
quick and energetic pressure on employers. The financial strength of workingmen when striking should not
be considered. Money may be supplied by contributions
of workingmen of other trades and localities, in itself
another means of developing the solidarity of the working-class. Sometimes a strike may be won by calling
out sympathetic strikes in other trades.

Strikes conducted in this manner yield practical results and serve also as means of educating the workingmen. They reveal to the workingmen their power, as
producers, and their importance in the productive system of society. The label, on the other hand, is a means
of bringing home to the workingmen their importance
as consumers, and of making them wield this power for
their own benefit.

The boycott reveals the power of the workingmen,
either as producers or as consumers. It may be wielded
against an employer whose shop is avoided, or against a
firm in its capacity as seller. It is an effective means of
forcing employers to terms.

Sabotage consists in obstructing in all possible ways
the regular process of production to the dismay and

disadvantage of the employer.   The manifestations of *sabotage* are many, varying with the nature of the industry and with the ingenuity of the workers.   In its primitive form, *sabotage* is a tacit refusal on the part of the workers to exert properly their energy or skill in the performance of their work, in retaliation for any injustice which, in their opinion, had been inflicted upon them by their employers. This form of *sabotage* includes such practices as those summarized in the Scotch *Ca Canny* (slow work for low wages) and in the French principle of *a mauvaise paye mauvais travail* (bad work for bad pay).   It also includes the recent practices of the railroad workers in Austria, Italy, and France who disorganized the railway service of their respective countries by obeying literally all the rules and regulations of the service code and by refusing to apply discretion and common sense in the performance of their duties.   The distinguishing characteristic of this form of *sabotage* is that in applying it the workers remain within the limits of their contract and avoid any manifest violation of the law, though the loss inflicted upon the employer may be very heavy.

A more aggressive form of *sabotage* is that which expresses itself in deliberate damage done either to the product of labor or to the nature of the service.   An instance of the latter was the so-called *grève perlée* applied by the French railway men, which consisted in wilful misdirection of baggage and of perishable merchandise. This form of sabotage implies disregard for the laws of property and for the clauses of the labor contract, but it is carried on in a manner which makes detection of motive very difficult.[1]

---

[1] An intermediate form of *sabotage* is that known as *sabotage à bouche ouverte* (sabotage of the open mouth).   It consists in the disclosure of

From this form of *sabotage* it is but a short step to the most aggressive and violent kind which finds expression in the deliberate and open disorganization of machinery. This form of *sabotage* has nothing in common with the destruction of machinery practiced by unorganized workers during the early stages of the capitalist régime. It aims not at the destruction of the machine as a means of production, but at the temporary disability of the machine during strikes for the purpose of preventing employers to carry on production with the help of strikebreakers. Even in this most aggressive form, *sabotage* may involve very little violence. The syndicalists strongly condemn any act of *sabotage* which may result in the loss of life.

Such are the "direct" methods of struggle against employers. But the revolutionary syndicalists have another enemy, the State, and the struggle against the latter is another aspect of "direct action."

The State appears to the syndicalists as the political organization of the capitalist class. Whether monarchist, constitutional, or republican, it is one in character, an organization whose function it is to uphold and to protect the privileges of the property-owners against the demands of the working-class. The workingmen are, therefore, necessarily forced to hurl themselves against the State in their efforts toward emancipation, and they cannot succeed until they have broken the power of the State.

The struggle against the State, like the struggle against the employers, must be carried on directly by

conditions generally withheld from the public, such as conditions in hotel-kitchens and restaurants, methods of weighing and measuring in stores, practices followed by druggists, frauds resorted to by contractors and builders, etc.

the workingmen themselves. This excludes the participation of the syndicats in politics and in electoral campaigning. The parliamentary system is a system of
representation opposed in principle to "direct action,"
and serves the interests of the bourgeoisie, for the management of which it is particularly suited. The workingmen can derive no benefit from it. The parliamentary system breeds petty, self-seeking politicians,
corrupts the better elements that enter into it and is a
source of intrigues and of "wire-pulling. The so-called
representatives of the workingmen do not and cannot
avoid the contagious influence of parliament. Their
policy degenerates into bargaining, compromising and
collaboration with the bourgeois political parties and
weakens the class-struggle.

The syndicats, therefore, if not hostile, must remain at
least indifferent to parliamentary methods and independent of political parties. They must, however, untiringly pursue their direct struggle against the State.
The direct method of forcing the State to yield to the
demands of the workingmen consists in exerting external pressure on the public authorities. Agitation in
the press, public meetings, manifestations, demonstrations and the like, are the only effective means of making the government reckon with the will of the working-class.

By direct pressure on the government the workingmen may obtain reforms of immediate value to themselves. Only such reforms, gained and upheld by force,
are real. All other reforms are but a dead letter and a
means of deceiving the workingmen.

The democratic State talks much about social reforms,
labor legislation and the like. In fact, however, all
labor laws that are of real importance have been passed

only under the pressure of the workingmen. Those which owe their existence to democratic legislators alone are devised to weaken the revolutionary strength of the working-class. Among such laws are those on conciliation and arbitration. All democratic governments are anxious to have Boards of Conciliation and of Arbitration, in order to check strikes which are the main force of the working-class. Workingmen must be opposed to these reforms, which are intended to further the harmony and collaboration of classes, because the ideology of class-harmony is one of the most dangerous snares which are set for the workingmen in a democratic State.[1] This ideology blinds the workingmen to the real facts of inequality and of class-distinctions which are the very foundations of existing society. It allures them into hopes which cannot be fulfilled and leads them astray from the only path of emancipation which is the struggle of classes.

Another idea which is used by the democratic State for the same purpose is the idea of patriotism. "Our country", "our nation", are mottoes inculcated into the mind of the workingman from his very childhood. But these words have no meaning for the workingman. The workingman's country is where he finds work. In search of work he leaves his native land and wanders from place to place. He has no fatherland (*patrie*) in any real meaning of the term. Ties of tradition, of a common intellectual and moral heritage do not exist for him. In his experience as workingman he finds that there is but one real tie, the tie of economic interest which binds him to all the workingmen of the world, and separates him at the same time from all the capitalists of the world. The in-

[1] The fundamental principle of democracy is that all citizens are equal before the law and that there are no classes in the state.

ternational solidarity of the workingmen and their anti-patriotism are necessary consequences of the class struggle.

The democratic State, like any other State, does not rely upon ideological methods alone in keeping down the workingmen. It has recourse to brute force as well. The judiciary, the administrative machinery and especially the army are used as means of defeating the movements of the working-class. The army is particularly effective as a means of breaking strikes, of crushing the spirit of independence in the workingmen, and as a means of keeping up the spirit of militarism. An anti-militaristic propaganda is therefore, one of the most important forms of struggle against the State, as well as against capitalism.

Anti-militarism consists in carrying on in the army a propaganda of syndicalist ideas. The soldiers are reminded that they are workingmen in uniforms, who will one day return to their homes and shops, and who should not, therefore, forget the solidarity which binds them to their fellow workingmen in blouses. The soldiers are called upon not to use their arms in strikes, and in case of a declaration of war to refuse to take up arms. The syndicalists threaten in case of war to declare a general strike. They are ardent apostles of international peace which is indispensable, in their opinion, to the success of their movement.

By "direct action" against employers and the State the workingmen may wrest from the ruling classes reforms which may improve their condition more or less. Such reforms can not pacify the working class because they do not alter the fundamental conditions of the wage system, but they are conducive to the fortification of the working-class and to its preparation for the final struggle. Every successful strike, every effective boycott, every manifestation of the workingmen's will and power is a blow directed against the existing order; every gain in wages, every shortening of hours of work, every improvement in the general conditions of employment is one more position of importance occupied on the march to the decisive battle, the general strike, which will be the final act of emancipation.

The general strike—the supreme act of the class-war —will abolish the classes and will establish new forms of society. The general strike must not be regarded as a *deus ex machina* which will suddenly appear to solve all difficulties, but as the logical outcome of the syndicalist movement, as the act that is being gradually prepared by the events of every day. However remote it may appear, it is not a Utopia and its possibility cannot be refuted on the ground that general strikes have failed in the past and may continue to fail in the future. The failures of to-day are building the success of to-morrow, and in time the hour of the successful general strike will come.

What are the forms of the social organization which will take the place of those now in existence? The Congress of Lyons (1901) had expressed the wish to have this question on the program of the next Congress. In order that the answer to this question should reflect the ideas prevalent among the workingmen, the Confederal Committee submitted the question to the syndicats for study. A questionnaire was sent out containing the following questions:

(1) How would your syndicat act in order to transform itself from a group for combat into a group for production?

(2) How would you act in order to take possession of the machinery pertaining to your industry?

(3) How do you conceive the functions of the organized shops and factories in the future?

(4) If your syndicat is a group within the system of highways, of transportation of products or of passengers, of distribution, etc., how do you conceive its functioning?

(5) What will be your relations to your federation of trade or of industry after your reorganization?

(6) On what principle would the distribution of products take place and how would the productive groups procure the raw material for themselves?

(7) What part would the *Bourses du Travail* play in the transformed society and what would be their task with reference to the statistics and to the distribution of products?

At the Congress of Montpellier, in 1902, a number of reports were presented answering the above questions. The reports were in the name of the syndicats and came from different parts of France. Only a limited number of them were printed as appendices to the general report of the Congress. Among them, it may be interesting to note, was the report of the syndicat of agricultural laborers. The rest were summed up in the official organ of the Confederation, *La Voix du Peuple*.

The reports differed in details. Some emphasized one point more than another and *vice versa*. But the general character of the reports was identical and showed a consensus of opinion on the main outlines of that "economic federalism" which is the ideal of the syndicalists. According to this ideal, the syndicat will constitute the cell of society. It will group the producers of one and the same trade who will control their means of production. Property, however, will be social or collective, and no one syndicat will be the exclusive owner of any portion of the collective property. It will merely use it with the consent of the entire society.

The syndicat will be connected with the rest of society through its relations with the Federation of its trade, the *Bourse du Travail*, and the General Confederation. With the National Federation relations will be mainly technical and special, and the rôle of the Federation will be insignificant. With the General Confederation relations will be indirect and mainly by mediation of the *Bourse du Travail*. Relations with the latter will be of permanent importance, as the *Bourses du Travail* will be the centers of economic activity.

The *Bourse du Travail*—in the ideal system of the syndicalists—will concentrate all local interests and serve as a connecting link between a locality and the rest of the world. In its capacity as local center it will collect all statistical data necessary for the regular flow of economic life. It will keep itself informed on the necessities of the locality and on its resources, and will provide for the proper distribution of products; as intermediary between the locality and the rest of the country it will facilitate the exchange of products between locality and locality and will provide for the introduction of raw materials from outside.

In a word, the Bourse will combine in its organization the character both of local and of industrial autonomy. It will destroy the centralized political system of the present State and will counterbalance the centralizing tendencies of industry.

To the General Confederation will be left only services of national importance, railways for instance. However, even in the management of national public utilities the National Federation and the Bourses will have the first word. The function of the General Confederation will consist mainly in furnishing general information and in exerting a controlling influence. The General Confederation will also serve as intermediary in international relations.

In this social system the State as now constituted will have no place. Of course, one may call the ideal system of the syndicalists a State. All depends on the definition given to the term. But when the syndicalists speak of the State, they mean an organization of society in which a delegated minority centralizes in its hands the power of legislation on all matters. This power may be broken up and divided among a number of governing bodies, as in the federal system of the United States, but it does not thereby change its character. The essential characteristic of the State is to impose its rule *from without*. The legislative assemblies of the present State decide upon questions that are entirely foreign to them, with which they have no real connection in life and which they do not understand. The rules they prescribe, the discipline they impose, come as an external agency to intervene in the processes of social life. The State is, therefore, arbitrary and oppressive in its very nature.

To this State-action the syndicalists oppose a discipline coming *from within*, a rule suggested by the processes of collective life itself, and imposed by those whose function it is to carry on those processes. It is, as it were, a specialization of function carried over into the domain of public life and made dependent upon industrial specialization. No one should legislate on matters unless he has the necessary training. The syndicats, the delegates of the syndicats to the *Bourses du Travail*, and so on, only they can properly deal with their respective problems. The rules they would impose would follow from a knowledge of the conditions of their social functions and would be, so to speak, a "natural" discipline made inevitable by the conditions themselves. Besides, many of the functions of the existing State would be abolished as unnecessary in a society based on common ownership, on co-operative work, and on collective solidarity. The necessary functions of local administration would be carried on by the *Bourses du Travail*.

In recent years, however, revolutionary syndicalists have not expatiated upon the forms of the future society. Convinced that the social transformation is inevitable, they have not thought it necessary to have any ready-made model upon the lines of which the social organization of the future should be carved. The revolutionary classes of the past had no idea of the new social system they were struggling for, and no ready-made plan is necessary for the working-class. Prepared by all preliminary struggle, the workingmen will find in themselves, when the time comes, sufficient creative power to remake society. The lines of the future, however, are indicated in a general way by the development of the present, and the syndicalist movement is clearly paving the way for an "economic federalism".

The workingmen are being prepared for their future rôle by the experiences of syndicalist life. The very struggle which the syndicats carry on train the workingmen in solidarity, in voluntary discipline, in power and determination to resist oppression, and in other moral qualities which group life requires. Moreover, the syndicats, particulary the *Bourses du Travail*, are centers where educational activities are carried on. Related to the facts of life and to the concrete problems of the day, this educational work, in the form of regular courses, lectures, readings, etc., is devised to develop the intellectual capacities of the workingmen.

The struggle of the present and the combat of the future imply the initiative, the example and the leadership of a conscious and energetic minority ardently devoted to the interests of its class. The experience of the labor movement has proven this beyond all doubt. The mass of workinmen, like every large mass, is inert. It needs an impelling force to set it in motion and to put to work its tremendous potential energy. Every strike, every labor demonstration, every movement of the working-class is generally started by an active and daring minority which voices the sentiments of the class to which it belongs.

The conscious minority, however, can act only by carrying with it the mass, and by making the latter participate directly in the struggle. The action of the conscious minority is, therefore, just the opposite of the action of parliamentary representatives. The latter are bent on doing everything themselves, on controlling absolutely the affairs of the country, and are therefore, anxious, to keep the massess as quiet, as inactive and as submissive as possible. The conscious minority, on the contrary, is simply the advance-guard of its class; it cannot succeed, unless backed by the solid forces of the masses; the awareness, the readiness and the energy of the latter are indispensable conditions of success and must be kept up by all means.

The idea of the "conscious minority" is opposed to the democratic principle. Democracy is based upon majority-rule, and its method of determining the general will is universal suffrage. But experience has shown that the "general will" is a fiction and that majority-rule really becomes the domination of a minority— which can impose itself upon all and exploit the majority in its own interests. This is inevitably so, because universal suffrage is a clumsy, mechanical device, which brings together a number of disconnected units and makes them act without proper understanding of the thing they are about. The effect of political majorities when they do make themselves felt is to hinder advance and to suppress the progressive, active and more developed minorities.

The practice of the labor movement is necessarily the reverse of this. The syndicats do not arise out of universal suffrage and are not the representatives of the majority in the democratic sense of the term. They group but a minority of all workingmen and can hardly expect ever to embrace the totality or even the majority of the latter. The syndicats arise through a process of selection. The more sensitive, the intellectually more able, the more active workingmen come together and constitute themselves a syndicat. They begin to discuss the affairs of their trade. • When determined to obtain its demands, the syndicat enters into a struggle, without at first finding out the "general will." It assumes leadership and expects to be followed, because it is convinced that it expresses the feelings of all. The syndicat constitutes the leading conscious minority.

The syndicat obtains better conditions not for its members alone, but for all the members of the trade and often for all the workingmen of a locality or of the country. This justifies its self-assumed leadership, because it is not struggling for selfish ends, but for the interests of all. Besides, the syndicat is not a medieval guild and is open to all. If the general mass of workingmen do not enter the syndicats, they themselves renounce the right of determining conditions for the latter. Benefiting by the struggles of the minority, they cannot but submit to its initiative and leadership.

The syndicat, therefore, is not to be compared with "cliques," "rings," "political machines," and the like. The syndicat, it must be remembered, is a group of individuals belonging to the same trade. By this very economic situation, the members of a syndicat are bound by ties of common interest with the rest of their fellow-workingmen. A sense of solidarity and an altruistic feeling of devotion to community interests must necessarily arise in the syndicat which is placed in the front ranks of the struggling workingmen. The leadership of the syndicalist minority, therefore, is necessarily disinterested and beneficent and is followed voluntarily by the workingmen.

Thus, grouping the active and conscious minority the syndicats lead the workingmen as a class in the struggle for final emancipation. Gradually undermining the foundations of existing society, they are developing within the framework of the old the elements of a new society, and when this process shall have sufficiently advanced, the workingmen rising in the general strike will sweep away the undermined edifice and erect the new society born from their own midst.

CHAPTER VI

The Theorists of Revolutionary Syndicalism

THE writers who have contributed to the development of revolutionary syndicalism may be divided into two groups. One comprises men who, like Pelloutier, Pouget, Griffuelhes, Delesalle, Niel, Yvetot and others, either belong to the working-class, or have completely identified themselves with the workingmen. The other consists of a number of "intellectuals" who stand outside of the syndicalist movement.

The members of the first group have played the leading part in building up the syndicalist movement. Pelloutier was secretary of the Federation of Bourses from 1894 to 1901; Griffuelhes was secretary of the General Confederation of Labor from 1901 to 1908; Pouget was assistant secretary of the Confederation and editor of the *Voix du Peuple* from 1900 to 1908; Yvetot has been one of the secretaries of the Confederation since 1902; Niel was secretary of the General Confederation for a short time in 1909, and the others now occupy or have occupied prominent places in the syndicalist organizations.

The close connection of the members of this group with the syndicalist movement and with the General Confederation of Labor has had its influence upon their writings. Their ideas have been stimulated by close observation of the facts of syndicalist life, and the course of their thought has been determined largely by the

struggles of the day. There is a stronger emphasis in
their writings upon methods, upon " direct action," and
upon relations to other existing groups. There is less
speculation and pure theorizing. In other respects the
men of this group differ. They have come from different political groupings : Pouget and Yvetot, for instance,
from the Communist-Anarchists; Griffuelhes from the
Allemanists. They have different views on the relation
of revolutionary syndicalism to other social theories,
differences which will be brought out further on.

The second group of writers, the so-called "intellectuals " outside the syndicalist movement, have grouped
themselves about the monthly *Le Mouvement Socialiste*,
started in 1899 by M. Hubert Lagardelle, a member of
the Socialist Party, and about the weekly *La Guerre
Sociale*, of which Gustave Hervé is editor. *Le Mouvement Socialiste* was at first a Socialist monthly review,
but accentuated its sympathy for the syndicalists as time
went on, and became an expressly revolutionary syndicalist organ in 1904. The *Mouvement Socialiste* counted
among its constant contributors down to 1910 M.
Georges Sorel and Edouard Berth. These three writers,
Sorel, Lagardelle, and Berth, have tried to systematize
the ideas of revolutionary syndicalism and to put them
on a philosophical and sociological basis. The most
prolific of them and the one who has been proclaimed
"the most profound thinker of the new school" is M.
Georges Sorel.

M. Georges Sorel has written on various subjects.
Among the works from his pen are volumes on Socrates,
on *The Historical System of Renan*, on *The Ruin of the
Ancient World*, a number of articles on ethics and on
various other topics. The works that bear on revolutionary syndicalism which alone can be here considered,

are: *L'Avenir Socialiste des Syndicats, La Décomposition du Marxisme, Introduction à l'Économie Moderne, Les Illusions du Progrès, Réflexions sur la Violence,* and a number of articles in various periodicals.

The works of M. Sorel on revolutionary syndicalism stretch over a period of ten to twelve years : *The Socialist Future of the Syndicats* was written in 1897; the second edition of his *Reflections on Violence* appeared in 1910. Within this period of time the thought of M. Sorel has not only steadily developed in scope but has also changed in many essential points. It would require a separate study to point out the changes and their significance. This is out of the question in this study. The salient points only of M. Sorel's theories will be treated here, therefore, without consideration of their place in the intellectual history of their author.

M. Sorel has attached his theories to the ideas of Marx. Revolutionary syndicalism is to M. Sorel but the revival and further development of the fundamental ideas of Marx. The "new school" considers itself, therefore, "neo-Marxist," true to "the spirit" of Marx[1] though rejecting the current interpretations of Marx and completing the lacunae which it finds in Marx. This work of revision it considers indispensable because, on the one hand, Marx was not always "well inspired,"[2] and often harked back to the past instead of penetrating into the future; and because, on the other hand, Marx did not know all the facts that have now become known; Marx knew well the development of the bourgeoisie, but could not know the development of the labor movement which has become such a tremendous factor in social life.[3]

[1] G. Sorel, *L'Avenir Socialiste des Syndicats* (Paris, 1901), p. 3.
[2] G. Sorel, *Réflexions sur la Violence* (Paris, 1910), p. 249.
[3] *Ibid.*, p. 246.

The "new school" does not consider itself by any means bound to admire "the illusions, the faults, the errors of him who has done so much to elaborate the revolutionary ideas."[1]   What it retains of Marx is his essential and fruitful idea of social evolution, namely, that the development of each social system furnishes the material conditions for effective and durable changes in the social relations within which a new system begins its development.[2]   Accordingly, Socialists must drop all utopian ideas : they must understand that Socialism is to be developed gradually in the bosom of capitalism itself and is to be liberated from within capitalistic surroundings only when the time is ripe.

The ripening of socialism within capitalism does not mean merely technical development.   This is indispensable of course : socialism can be only an economic system based on highly developed and continually progressing productive forces ; but this is one aspect of the case only.   The other, a no less if not more important aspect, is the development of new moral forces within the old system ; that is, the political, juridical and moral development of the working-class,[3] of that class which alone can establish a socialist society.

This was also the idea of Marx : "Marx also saw that the workingmen must acquire political and juridical capacity before they can triumph."[4]   The revolution which the working-class is pursuing is not a simple change in the personnel or in the form of the government ; it is a complete overthrow of the "traditional State" which is to be replaced by the workingmen's organizations. Such a complete transformation presupposes "high moral

[1] G. Sorel, *Réflexions sur la Violence* (Paris, 1910), p. 249.
[2] G. Sorel, *L' Avenir Socialiste des Syndicats*, pp. 3-4.
[3] *Ibid.*, p. 39.   [4] *Ibid.*, p. 4.

culture " in the workingmen and a capacity for directing *educate*
the economic functions of society.⌠ The social revolution
will thus come only when the workingmen are "ready"
for it, that is, when they feel that they can assume the
direction of society.   The "moral" education of the
working class, therefore, is the essential thing; Socialism
will not have to "organize labor", because capitalism
will have accomplished this work before.   But in order
that the working-class should be able to behave like "free
men" in the "workshop created by capitalism",[1] they
must have developed the necessary capacities.   Socialism,
therefore, reduces itself "to the revolutionary apprenticeship"[2] of the workingmen; "to teaching the workingmen to will, to instructing them by action, and to revealing to them their proper capacities; such is the whole
secret of the socialist education of the people."[3]

The workingmen can find the moral training necessary
for the triumph of socialism only in the syndicats and in
the experience of syndical life.   The syndicats develop
the administrative and organizing capacities of the workingmen.   In the syndicats the workingmen learn to do
their business themselves and to reject the dictatorship
of "intellectuals" who have conquered the field of politics which they have made to serve their ambitions.

The greatest organizing and educating force created
by the syndicalist movement is the idea of the general
strike.   The general strike means a complete and "absolute" revolution.   It is the idea of a decisive battle
between the bourgeoisie and the working-class assuring
the triumph of the latter.   This idea is a "social myth"
and hence its tremendous historic force.

---

[1] G. Sorel, *Réflexions sur la Violence*, pp. 289-5.   [2] *Ibid.*, p. 42.
[3] G. Sorel, *Préface* to Pelloutier's *Histoire des Bourses du Travail*.

"Social myths" always arise during great social movements. The men who participate in great social movements, represent to themselves their actions in the near
future in the form of images of battles assuring the triumph of their cause. These images are "myths." The
images of the early Christians on the coming of Christ
and on the ruin of the pagan world are an illustration of
a "social myth." The period of the Reformation saw
the rise of "social myths," because the conditions were
such as to make it necessary for the "men of heart"
who were inspired by "the will of deliverance" to create
"images" which satisfying their "sentiments of struggle"
kept up their zeal and their devotion.

The "social myth" presupposes a social group which
harbors an intense desire of deliverance, which feels all
the difficulties in its way and which finds deep satisfaction in picturing to itself its future struggles and future
triumph. Such images must not and cannot be analyzed
like a thing; they must be taken *en bloc*, and it is particularly necessary to avoid comparing the real historic
facts with the representations which were in circulation
before the facts took place.

"Myths" are indispensable for a revolutionary movement; they concentrate the force of the rising class and
intensify it to the point of action. No myth can possibly be free from utopian conceptions. But the utopian
elements are not essential. The essentials are the hope
back of the myth, the ideal strengthened by the myth,
and the impatience of deliverance embodied in the myth.

The general strike is the "social myth" of the working-class longing for emancipation. It is the expression
of the convictions of the working-class "in the language
of movement," the supreme concentration of the desires,
the hopes, and the ideals of the working-class. Its im-

portance for the future of Socialism, therefore, is para-
mount. The idea of the general strike keeps alive and
fortifies in the workingmen their class-consciousness
and revolutionary feelings. Every strike on account of
it assumes the character of a skirmish before the great
decisive battle which is to come. Owing to the general
strike idea, "socialism remains ever young, the attempts
made to realize social peace seem childish, the desertion
of comrades who run over into the ranks of the bourgeoisie, far from discouraging the masses, excites them
still more to revolt; in a word, the rupture (between
bourgeoisie and working-class) is never in danger of
disappearing."[1]

This rupture is an indispensable condition of Socialism. Socialism cannot be the continuation of democracy; it must be, if it can be at all, a totally "new culture" built upon ideas and institutions totally different
from the ideas and from the institutions of democracy.
Socialism must have its own economic, judicial, political
and moral institutions evolved by the working-class independently from those of the bourgeoisie, and not in
imitation of the latter.

Sorel is bitter in his criticism of democracy; it is, in
his view, the régime *par excellence* in which men are
governed "by the magical power of high-sounding words
rather than by ideas; by formulas rather than by reasons;
by dogmas the origin of which nobody cares to find out,
rather than by doctrines based on observation."[2] It is
the kingdom of the professionals of politics, over whom
the people can have no control. Sorel thinks that even
the spread of knowledge does not render the masses

[1] G. Sorel, *Réflexions sur la Violence*, p. 179.
[2] G. Sorel, *Illusions du progrès* (Paris, 1911), p. 10.

more capable of choosing and of supervising their so-
called representatives and that the further society ad-
vances in the path of democracy, the less effective does
control by the people become.[1] The whole system of
democracy, in the opinion of M. Sorel, is based on the
"fiction of the general will" and is maintained by a
mechanism (campaigning, elections, etc.) which can result only in demoralization. It delivers the country into
the hands of "charlatans," of office-seekers and of idle
talkers who may assume the air of great men, but who
are never fit for their task.

The working-class must, therefore, break entirely with
democracy and evolve from within itself its own ideas
and original institutions. This complete rupture between the ideas of the past and those of the future con-
tradicts the conception of progress now in vogue. But
the conception of progress is rather a deception than a
conception. As held to-day, it is full of illusions, of
errors, and of misconceptions. The idea of progress is
characteristic of democracy and is cherished by the bourgeois classes because it permits them to enjoy their privileges in peace. Lulled by the optimistic illusion that
everything is for the best in this best of all worlds, the
privileged classes can peacefully and hopefully pass by
the misery and the disorders of existing society. This
conception of progress, like all other ideas of democracy,
was evolved by the rising middle classes of the eigh-
teenth century, mainly by the functionaries of royalty
who furnished the theoretical guides of the Revolution.
But, in truth, the only real progress is the development
of industrial technique[2]—the constant invention of machinery and the increase of productive forces. The latter

[1] G. Sorel, *Illusions du Progrès*, p. 59.   [2] *Ibid.*, p. 276.

create the material conditions out of which a new culture arises, completely breaking with the culture of the past.

One of the factors promoting the development of productive forces is "proletarian violence." This violence is not to be thought of after the model of the "Reign of Terror" which was the creation of the bourgeoisie. "Proletarian violence" does not mean that there should be a "great development of brutality" or that "blood should be shed in torrents" (*versé à flots*).[1] It means that the workingmen in their struggle must manifest their force so as to intimidate the employers; it means that "the social conflicts must assume the character of pure struggles similar to those of armies in a campaign."[2] Such violence will show the capitalist class that all their efforts to establish social peace are useless; the capitalists will then turn to their economic interests exclusively; the type of a forceful, energetic "captain of industry" will be the result, and all the possibilities of capitalism will be developed.

On the other hand, violence stimulates ever anew the class-feelings of the workingmen and their sentiments of the sublime mission which history has imposed upon them. It is necessary that the revolutionary syndicalists should feel that they are fulfiling the great and sublime mission of renovating the world; this is their only compensation for all their struggles and sufferings. The feelings of sublimity and enthusiasm have disappeared from the bourgeois-world, and their absence has contributed to the decadence of the bourgeoisie. The working-class is again introducing these feelings by incorporating them in the idea of the general strike, and is, therefore, making possible a moral rejuvenation of the world.

---

[1] G. Sorel, *Réflexions sur la Violence*, pp. 256-7.   [2] *Ibid.*, p. 150.

All these ideas may seem tinged with pessimism. But "nothing very great (*très haut*) has been accomplished in this world" without pessimism.[1] Pessimism is a "metaphysics of morals" rather than a theory of the world; it is a conception of "a march towards deliverance" and presupposes an experimental knowledge of the obstacles in the way of our imaginings or in other words "a sentiment of social determinism" and a feeling of our human weakness.[2] The pessimist "regards social conditions as forming a system enchained by an iron law, the necessity of which must be submitted to as it is given *en bloc*, and which can disappear only after a catastrophe involving the whole."[3] This catastrophic character the general strike has and must have, if it is to retain its profound significance.

The catastrophic character of the general strike enhances its moral value. The workingmen are stimulated by it to prepare themselves for the final combat by a moral effort over themselves. But only in such unique moments of life when "we make an effort to create a new man within ourselves" "do we take possession of ourselves" and become free in the Bergsonian sense of the term. /The general strike, therefore, raises socialism to the rôle of the greatest moral factor of our time.\

Thus, M. Sorel having started out with Marx winds up with Bergson. The attempt to connect his views with the philosophy of Bergson has been made by M. Sorel in all his later works. But all along M. Sorel claims to be "true to the spirit of Marx" and tries to prove this by various quotations from the works of Marx. It is doubtful, however, whether there is an

---

[1] G. Sorel, *Réflexions sur la Violence*, p. 8.
[2] *Ibid.*, p. 12.   [3] *Ibid.*, p. 13.

affinity between the "spirit" of Marx and that of Professor Bergson. It appears rather that M. Sorel has tacitly assumed this affinity because he interprets the "spirit" of Marx in a peculiar and arbitrary way.

Without any pretense of doing full justice to the subject, three essential points may be indicated which perhaps sufficiently prove that "neo-Marxism" has drifted so far away from Marx as to lose touch with his "spirit." These three points bear upon the very kernel of Marxism: its conception of determinism, its intellectualism, and its emphasis on the technical factors of social evolution.

The Marxian conception of social determinism is well known. The social process was thought of by Marx as rigidly "necessary," as an organic, almost as a mechanical process. The impression of social necessity one gets in reading Marx is so strong as to convey the feeling of being carried on by an irresistible process to a definite social end.

In M. Sorel's works, on the contrary, social determinism is a word merely, the concept back of it is not assimilated. M. Sorel speaks of the general strike and of Socialism as of possibilities or probabilities, not of necessities. In reading him, one feels that M. Sorel himself never felt the irresistible character of the logical category of necessity.

The difference in the second point follows from the difference in the first. Marx never doubted the possibility of revealing the secret of the social process. Trained in the "panlogistic school," Marx always tacitly assumed that socialism could be scientific, that the procedure of science could prove the necessity of social evolution going in one direction and not in any other. It was the glory of having given this proof which he claimed for himself and which has been claimed for him by his disciples.

M. Sorel is expressly not "true to the spirit" of Marx in this point. "Science has no way of foreseeing,"[1] says he. His works are full of diatribes against the pretention of science to explain everything. He attributes a large rôle to the unclear, to the subconscious and to the mystical in all social phenomena. A sentence like the following may serve to illustrate this point. Says M. Sorel:

> Socialism is necessarily a very obscure thing, because it treats of production—that is, of what is most mysterious in human activity—and because it proposes to realize a radical transformation in this region which it is impossible to describe with the clearness which is found in the superficial regions of the world. (No effort of thought, no progress of knowledge, no reasonable induction will ever be able to dispel the mystery which envelops Socialism.[2])

This, according to Sorel, is just what "Marxism has recognized": M. Sorel, certainly, "knows his Marx."

In the third point, M. Sorel "the revolutionary revisionist," comes very close to M. Bernstein, "the evolutionary revisionist." The coming of Socialism is made independent of those technical and economic processes which Marx so much emphasized. The conceptions of the concentration of capital, of proletarization, etc., are given up. On the contrary, Socialism is to be prepared by the "revolutionary apprenticeship" of the working-class, an apprenticeship to be made in action and under the influence of a "social myth" created by imagination

[1] G. Sorel, *L'Avenir Socialiste des Syndicats*, p. 54.
[2] G. Sorel, *Réflexions sur la Violence*, pp. 201-2.

spurred on by the subconscious will. There certainly
are pronounced voluntaristic elements in Marx, but this
whole conception of M. Sorel seems to attribute to Marx
a "spirit" by no means in harmony with his make-up.

Though claiming to be a disciple of Marx, M. Sorel
seems to be more in harmony with Proudhon whose
works he often quotes and whose views, particularly
on morals, he accepts. But besides Proudhon many
other writers have had a considerable influence on
M. Sorel. Besides Bergson, already mentioned, Renan
and Nietzsche, to quote but two, have had their share of
influence in many of the ideas expressed by M. Sorel.
M. Sorel has an essentially mobile mind quick to catch
an idea and to give it a somewhat new and original turn.
He lacks the ability of systematizing his views and his
reader must have considerable patience with him. The
systematic way in which his views have been given in
this chapter is rather misleading; M. Sorel himself pro-
ceeds in a quite different way; he deals with an idea for
a while but is led away into digression after digression,
to pick up the thread of his previous argument tens of
pages later.

Lack of system makes it easier for contradictions to
live together without detection. It also predisposes a
writer to assimilate and to transform any ideas he may
meet. With Sorel this is evidently so, though his main
claim is "profundity." The pages of his work bristle
with the word *approfondir* which is so often repeated
that it makes the poor reader dizzy. The disappointment is sharp, because M. Sorel soon loses the thread
of his thought before having had time to fathom his subject. His works, however, savor of freshness of thought
and of originality.

Quite a different writer is M. Lagardelle. His ex-

position is regular, systematic, fluent, and clear. While
Sorel is mainly interested in the philosophical aspect of
his problems and has been called, probably sarcastically,
by M. Jaures " the metaphysician of revolutionary syndicalism," M. Lagardelle considers the economic and
political aspects of the new doctrine. His works need
not be dwelt upon because his ideas do not differ essentially from those of M. Sorel. Two points, however,
may be singled out ; M. Lagardelle, though criticizing
democracy, is careful to point out that Socialism has
been made possible by democracy and that no return to
ancient political forms is desired ; secondly, he allows a
place for the political [socialist] party in the general
social system; its rôle is to attend to those problems
which are not entirely included within the domain of industrial activities.[1]

While the " Mouvement Socialiste " devoted its attention mainly to the philosophical and sociological aspects
of syndicalism, the weekly *La Guerre Sociale* took up
questions of policy and method, particularly the questions of anti-militarism and anti-patriotism. Gustave
Hervé, the editor of the paper, attracted widespread
attention by his attacks on the army and on the idea of
patriotism, and became the *enfant terrible* of the French
socialist movement because of his violent utterances on
these questions. On other questions of method, M.
Hervé was no less violent being a disciple of the Blanquists who believed in the efficacy of all revolutionary
methods including the general strike. However, the
theoretical contributions of M. Hervé to the philosophy
of the movement are slight.

Now, what are the relations of the two groups of

[1] H. Lagardelle, *Le Socialisme Ouvrier* (Paris, 1911).

writers described in this chapter and what part has each played in the history of the movement? These questions must be carefully considered if a correct understanding of revolutionary syndicalism is desired.

The view which prevailed outside of France is that M. Sorel and his disciples "created" the theory of revolutionary socialism in opposition to the parliamentary socialists, and that they have been able to impress their ideas upon a larger or smaller portion of the organized French workingmen. This view was first presented by Professor W. Sombart in his well-known work on *Socialism and the Social Movement,* and has made its way into other writings on revolutionary syndicalism. M. Sorel is often spoken of as the "leader" of the revolutionary syndicalists, and the whole movement is regarded as a form of Marxian revisionism.

This view, however, is a "myth" and should be discarded. French writers who have studied the social movement of their country and who are competent judges have tried to dispel the error that has gotten abroad.[1] The theorists of the *Movement Socialiste* themselves have repeatedly declined the "honor" which error has conferred upon them. M. Lagardelle has reiterated time and again that revolutionary syndicalism was born of the experience of the labor movement and worked out by the workingmen themselves. M. Sorel has said that he learned more from the syndicalist workingmen than they could learn from him. And in an article reviewing the book of Professor Sombart, M. Berth has insisted that Professor Sombart was in error. "If we had any part," wrote he, "it was the simple part of interpreters, of translators, of glossers; we have served as

[1] See articles of Lagardelle, G. Weil and Cornelissen in the *Archiv für Sozialwissenchaft und Sozialpolitik,* 1907-1910.

spokesmen, that's all; but it is necessary to avoid reducing to a few propositions of a school, a movement which is so essentially working-class and the leading ideas of which, such as direct action and the general strike, are so specifically of a working-class character." [1]

This must not be taken as over-modesty on the part of "intellectuals" who are careful not to pose as leaders or as inspirers. The facts are there to prove the statements of M. Lagardelle and of M. Sorel. The idea of the general strike was elaborated by workingmen-members of the various committees on the general strike. The idea of "direct action," as has been shown, found its defenders in the first Congresses of the General Confederation of Labor. The theory of the social rôle of the syndicat was formulated by Pelloutier and by other members of the "Federation of Bourses" before M. Sorel wrote his little book on *The Socialist Future of the Syndicats*.

Even the statement of M. Berth must be somewhat modified. The theorists of the *Mouvement Socialiste* have never by any means been the authorized "spokesmen" of the revolutionary syndicalists of the General Confederation. They were no more than a group of writers who, watching the syndicalist movement from the outside, were stimulated by it to their reflections and ideas. They thought they found in the syndicalist movement "a truly original force capable of refreshing the socialist conception", and they formulated their ideas on the subject. They never took any part in the movement, and could not feel themselves its representatives.

What then was their influence? In general, the same as that of other socialist writers. They were and are

[1] *Les Mouvement Socialiste* (May, 1908), p. 390.

read by the French workingmen just as Kropotkin,
Jaures, Proudhon and other contemporary or former
socialist and anarchist writers, and as many non-socialist
writers are. Naturally, some workingmen came more
under their influence, than under that of others; and
such workingmen may be disposed to look upon them as
their theoretical guides and leaders.

But even the latter interpretation is by no means ap-
plicable to all the theories of M. Sorel, for the main ideas
of Sorel seem fundamentally incapable of inspiring a
movement of large masses. The theory of the "social
myth" may be original and attractive, but if accepted by
the workingmen could not inspire them to action. If
"images of battles" are important for the "rising
classes" as an impelling force, they can be so only so
long as they are naïvely and fully believed in. The worm
of reflection must not touch them. The "men longing
for deliverance" must believe that the future will be just
as they picture it, otherwise their enthusiasm for these
pictures would find no nourishment. Should they come
to realize the "utopian" and "mythical" character of
their constructions they would abandon them.

The pessimistic basis of M. Sorel's *Weltanschauung*
may appeal to literary men, to students of philosophy
and to individuals longing for a moral theory. It can
not be assimilated by a mass "moving toward emancipation." When one reads the original documents of the
syndicalist movement, he is struck, on the contrary, by
the powerful torrent of optimism by which the movement is carried along. Only a strong belief in a "speedy
emancipation" created the enthusiasm for the idea of the
general strike. There may be a subconscious pessimism
back of this optimism, but its appearance in the field of
clear consciousness would have been destructive for the
movement.

It is, therefore, quite natural that the writers representing the General Confederation of Labor who address the workingmen directly do not reproduce these theories of M. Sorel. As has been indicated already, their writings bear a different stamp. And if among these writers some, as for instance M. Griffuelhes, seem to have come more under the influence of the group *Le Mouvement Socialiste*, the rest occupy an independent position even from the theoretical point of view.

How little M. Sorel could have been the "leader" of the revolutionary syndicalist movement may be illustrated by the following comparison. At the Congress of Lyons in 1901 the secretary of the General Confederation of Labor, M. Guerard, wrote, as we have seen, that the Confederation is destined to transform society. In the same year, M. Sorel, in his preface to Pelloutier's *Histoire des Bourses du Travail*, wrote: "The Confederation of Labor appears to me to be destined to become an officious Council of Labor, and an academy of proletarian ideas, which will present its wishes to the government, as the large agricultural societies do." The history of the General Confederation of Labor since 1902, to be considered in the following chapter, will show that M. Sorel missed the point too far to be able to claim the title of "leader" whose function, presumably, is to point out the way and not to acknowledge it, after it has once been taken.

It is necessary to bear all this in mind in order to grasp the real character of revolutionary syndicalism. M. Sorel has recently renounced his revolutionary syndicalist ideas. In December, 1910, he wrote to the Italian revolutionary syndicalists who invited him to their Congress at Boulogne:

It seems to the author [of the *Reflections on Violence*] that syndicalism has not realized what was expected from it. Many hope that the future will correct the evils of the present hour ; but the author feels himself too old to live in distant hopes ; and he has decided to employ the remaining years of his life in the deepening (*approfundir*) of other questions which keenly interest the cultivated youth of France. [1]

Previous to that, M. Sorel and M. Berth had both promised collaboration in a so-called neo-monarchist monthly, *La Cité Francaise*, which, however, did not see the light. This probably seemed to them natural in view of their opposition to democracy. But under the political conditions of France such an act could not but shock the workingmen who may criticise democracy but who are bitterly opposed to everything connected with the *ancien régime*. This act of M. Sorel and M. Berth weakened the group of *Le Mouvement Socialiste* which, however, is still published by M. Lagardelle, though with less force and *éclat* than before. The act of M. Sorel, however, could have no perceptible significance for the revolutionary syndicalist movement. The latter is led by other leaders and is determined in its march by other influences.

The revolutionary syndicalist ideas embodied in the movement represented by the General Confederation of Labor were evolved, as has been shown, in the syndicalist organizations of France. The Anarchists entering the syndicats largely contributed to the revolutionary turn which the syndicats took. Their influence, hailed by some, deplored by others, is recognized by all. The Anarchists themselves often speak as if they "created" the entire movement, though this is an exaggeration. The rôle of the Allemanists has been considerable, as was shown in the preceding chapters. And the more definite

[1] *Le Mouvement Socialiste* (March, 1911), pp. 184-5.

formulation of revolutionary syndicalist ideas in the period of "Millerandism" was the work of revolutionary socialist workingmen of all brands—Allemanists, Anarchists, Blanquists and others.

This clears up the question of the relation of revolutionary syndicalism to other social theories. The theorists of the *Mouvement Socialiste* have proclaimed revolutionary syndicalism as a new social theory. They have been very persistent in trying to delimit their theoretical dominion from parliamentary socialism on the one hand, and from Anarchism on the other. From the latter particularly they wished to be separated, feeling as they did how dangerously close they came to it. Many workingmen have accepted this view, proud to proclaim that they have evolved a theory of their own—the theory of the working-class.

Others, however, have taken the correct point of view. They see that the main ideas of revolutionary syndicalism cannot be said to be new. They may all be found in the old "International Association of Workingmen," and especially in the writings of the Bakounist or federalist wing of that Association. If not the terms, the ideas on direct action, on the general strike, on the social rôle of the syndicat, and on the future "economic federalism" may all be found there more or less clearly stated.[1]

Revolutionary syndicalism appears then, from this point of view not as a new theory, but as a return to the old theories of the "International" in which the combined influence of Proudhon, Marx and Bakounin manifested itself. The formulation of revolutionary syndicalism, however, is not to any great degree a conscious return to old ideas, though this conscious factor had its

[1] J. Guillaume, *L'Internationale*, vols. i–iii; also Report of 7th Congress of "International" in Brussels in 1874.

part; Pelloutier, for instance, was expressly guided by the conceptions of Proudhon and Bakounin. References to the "International" are also frequent in the discussions of the Congresses of the General Confederation. The more important factors, however, were the conditions of the French syndical movement itself. The workingmen of different socialist groups meeting on the common ground of the syndicat had to attenuate their differences and to emphasize their common points. Thus, by a process of elimination and of mutual influence a common stock of ideas was elaborated which, absorbing the quintessence of all socialist theories, became what is known as revolutionary syndicalism. Its similarity to the ideas of the "International" is partly due to the fact that in the "International" similar conditions existed.

Mainly worked out in the practice of the syndicalist movement, the ideas of revolutionary syndicalism are also mainly determined in their further evolution by this practice. The ideas, therefore, must be judged in connection with the conditions in which they developed. These conditions will be further described in the following chapters.

CHAPTER VII

THE GENERAL CONFEDERATION OF LABOR SINCE 1902

BEFORE taking up the history of the Confederation after 1902, a general outline of the constitution adopted at Montpellier must be given. Passim will be indicated the changes that have been made since.

The General Confederation of Labor consists of National Federations of industries and trades,[1] of National Syndicats, of isolated single syndicats (in that case only if there is no national or regional federation of the trade, or if the federation does not adhere to the Confederation), and of *Bourses du Travail*, considered as local, departmental or regional central unions.[2]

---

[1] In 1906 the statutes were so modified as to admit no new trade federations. This was a decided step in the direction of the industrial form of organization.

[2] At the last congress of the Confederation which was held in Havre in September, 1912, a resolution was passed that the Bourses du Travail in each Department of France should form Departmental Unions (Unions Departmentales), and that on January 1, 1914, these Departmental Unions should take the place of the Bourses du Travail in the organization of the Confederation. The resolution has not yet been fully carried into effect, and the process of reorganization is still going on. When it is completed, the General Confederation of Labor will emerge with a more compact and centralized form of organization embracing Federations of industry, on the one hand, and Departmental Unions, on the other. The single Bourses will not disappear, and their functions will not be curtailed; but they will henceforth form the constituent elements of the more comprehensive Departmental Unions and will have no individual representation in the Confederal Committee. The reorganization was made necessary by the rapid growth of Bourses du Travail,

Every syndicat adhering to the Confederation must fulfil the condition of so-called "double adherence;" that is, it must belong to its national federation of industry or trade, and to the *Bourse du Travail* of its locality. Besides, every federation must have at least one subscription to the *Voix du Peuple*, which is the official organ of the Confederation. These conditions, however, were, and still are disregarded by a considerable number of syndicats.[1]

The General Confederation is represented by the Confederal Committee which is formed by delegates of the adhering organizations. Each organization is represented by one delegate in the Confederal Committee. This point should be noticed as it is the cause of struggle within the Confederation. It means that a large Federation has only one delegate and one vote in the Confederal Committee, just as another smaller Federation. The number of delegates in the Confederal Committee, however, is not always equal to the number of adhering organizations, because one delegate may represent as many as three organizations. The delegates must be workingmen who have been members of their syndicat for at least a year.

The General Confederation has five central organs; two sections and three commissions. The first section is called : " The Section of Federations of trades and of industries and of isolated syndicats;" the second is "The

the number of which far outstripped the number of Federations of industry and which thus controlled the policies of the Confederal Committee. The number of the Departmental Unions can not exceed eighty-seven (87), as there are but eighty-seven political subdivisions in France called Departments.

[1] E. Pouget, *Le Conſédération Générale du Travail* (Paris, 1908), p. 16.

Section of the Federation of *Bourses du Travail.*"[1]   The three commissions are (1) the Commission of the journal; (2) the Commission of strikes and of the general strike, and (3) the Commission of Control.

The two sections are autonomous in their internal affairs. The first section is formed by the delegates of the National Federations of trades and industries. They take the name of *Comité des Fédérations d'industries et de metiers.* This section appoints it own secretary, assistant secretary, treasurer, assistant treasurer, and archivist, who form the executive committee of the section. This section collects monthly from every adhering organization 40 centimes[2] for every hundred members, or for any fraction of a hundred; isolated syndicats pay five centimes monthly for each member.

The Sections of Federations of industries and trades is convened by its secretary and meets whenever necessary. Its functions are to promote the organization of new federations and to maintain relations between the adhering federations, It takes "all measures necessary for the maintenance of syndical action in the field of economic struggle." It also tries to induce isolated syndicats to join their *Bourses du Travail.*

The "Section of the Federation of *Bourses du Travail*" is formed by the delegates of the local, departmental and regional central unions. The delegates take the title of *Comité des Bourses du Travail.*[3] The section appoints its own secretary, assistant secretary,

---

[1] From Jan. 1, 1914, called the "Section of the Federation of Departmental Unions."

[2] Increased in 1909 to 60 centimes. For further increase see page 195.

[3] When the reorganization is completed, this section will consist of one delegate from each Departmental Union, who will form the *Comité des Unions Departmentales.* See note 2 on page 162.

treasurer, assistant treasurer, and archivist, and these five members form the executive committee of the second section. It collects from the *Bourses du Travail* 35 centimes monthly for each adhering syndicat.[1]

The second section promotes the creation of new *Bourses du Travail* and coördinates the activities of the adhering Bourses. Its functions embrace "everything that bears upon syndical administration and upon the moral education of the workingmen;" its task is to collect statistics of production, of consumption, of unemployment; to organize gratuitous employment bureaus, to watch the progress of labor legislation, etc. It also tries to induce single syndicats to join their national federations. This section also meets whenever necessary at the invitation of its secretary.

The Commission of the Journal is composed of twelve members, six from each section. It appoints its own secretary. The journal must be edited only by workingmen-members of the Confederation.

The Commission of strikes and of the general strike consists also of twelve members, six from each section, and appoints its own secretary. The functions of this commission are: to study the strike movement in all countries, to send speakers and organizers to, and to collect subscriptions in favor of workingmen on strike, to make propaganda for the general strike, and to promote "the penetration of this idea into the minds of organized workingmen." For this purpose the commission creates wherever possible sub-committees of the general strike. This commission has its own resources which consist of 50 per cent of all money collected by the sub-committees, and of 50 per cent

---

[1] Changed in 1909 to five centimes for each member per year.

of the assessments collected by both sections of the Confederation.

The Commission of Control is also formed of twelve members, six from each section; it verifies the financial reports of both sections and of the other two commissions. It appoints its own secretary.

The Confederal Committee is formed by the delegates of both sections. It meets every three months, except in extraordinary cases. It executes the decisions of the Congresses, intervenes in all issues concerning the working-class and decides upon all questions of a general character.

The Confederal Bureau [1] consists of thirteen members, of the ten members of the bureaus of both sections and of the three secretaries of the three commissions. The Confederal Bureau summons the Confederal Committee and executes the decisions of the latter. The secretary of the "Section of Federations" is the general secretary of the Confederation. The Confederal Bureau is renewed after every Congress, that is every two years, but functionaries whose terms have expired may be re-elected.

Article 37 of the statutes adopted read: " The General Confederation of Labor, based on the principles of federalism and of liberty, assures and respects the complete autonomy of the organizations which conform to the present statutes." The *Bourses du Travail* and the Federations of industries and of trades were, therefore, to pursue independently the activities that concerned them alone. The *Bourses du Travail* continued in the main the activities described in the third chapter. Their growth was steady both in number of organizations and

[1] Executive Committee.

in membership, as may be seen from the following table:

	Number of Bourses belonging to the Confederation of Labor.	Number of Syndicats in Bourses of Confederation.
1902	83	1,112
1904	110	1,349
1906	135	1,609
1908	157	2,028
1910	154	1,826
1912	153	

After 1906 Bourses of the same region or Department began to form regional and Departmental Unions in order to coördinate their activities and to influence larger groups of the working population. This has led to the process described above, which is transforming the basis of representation in the General Confederation of Labor.

In matters of administration the *Bourses du Travail* have made a step in advance since the early part of the century. They have succeeded in organizing the *viaticum* (aid to workingmen traveling from town to town in search of work) on a national basis, and have amplified their services as employment bureaus. They are now systematizing their statistical work by making monthly and quarterly reports on the state of employment in their locality, on strikes, on the growth of organization, and on other industrial matters of interest. Their financial situation has been considerably improved, and in a number of cities they have left the municipal buildings and have built their own "people's houses" (*maisons du peuple*).

Regard for matters of administration has not diminished the zeal of the Bourses for anti-militaristic propaganda. Most of them have organized in recent years the so-called *Sou du Soldat* (Soldier's Penny). They send financial aid to workingmen who are doing military service, invite them to the social gatherings of the syndicats, distribute syndicalist literature among them, and in all ways try to maintain in the soldiers a feeling of solidarity with the organized workers.

The Federations of industries and trades after 1902 concentrated their attention upon their particular trade and industrial interests. The story of these Federations is the story of organization, education, and strikes which can not be told here in detail.

While the Bourses and industrial federations attended to the particular, local and administrative interests of their respective organizations, the General Confederation of labor intervened or took the initiative in questions that interested all or a considerable part of all workingmen. The new statutes went into force on January 1, 1903. The elections secured the predominance of the revolutionary syndicalists in the Confederal Committee; Griffuelhes was elected secretary of the Confederation; Pouget, assistant; Yvetot, secretary of the Section of Bourses. In October of the same year the Confederal Committee was summoned to an extraordinary meeting to consider the question of the suppression of employment bureaus. This question had agitated a considerable part of the working-class for many years. The workingmen had protested time and again against the methods and procedure of these bureaus, and their protests had been found to be well founded by all who investigated the matter.[1]   The methods of the employment bureaus had been condemned in Parliament, and the Chamber had passed a bill to suppress the employment bureaus with idemnity in 1901-2.   The Senate, however, rejected it in February, 1902, and the question was dropped indefinitely.

The workingmen of the food-producing industries (*alimentation*) were particularly interested in the suppression of the employment bureaus.   In October, 1903, exasperated by the fact that twenty-five years of lobbying and of petitioning had produced no results, they decided to take the matter into their own hands.   October 29th, a "veritable riot" took place in the *Bourse du Travail* of Paris, the police used their arms, and many were wounded on both sides.[2]

The Confederal Committee decided to lend its help to the workingmen in the struggle.   It appointed a special committee to direct the movement.   The plan adopted was to carry on a wide agitation for some time and then to arrange protest-meetings on the same day in all industrial centers of France.   December 5, 1903, hundreds of meetings were held all over France, at which the same demand was made that the employment offices be abolished.   The meetings were arranged with the help of the *Bourses du Travail* which appear in all such cases as the centers of agitation.

November 5, 1903, the Chamber, by 495 votes against 14, voted a law suppressing the Employment Bureaus within a period of five years, with an indemnity of six million francs.   In February, 1904, the law passed the Senate with some modifications.

[1] Senator Paul Straus in *La Grande Revue* (Feb., 1914), pp. 320 *et seq.*

[2] *Journal des Débats* (Nov. 6, 1903), p. 865.

The agitation for the suppression of the employment bureaus appeared to all as a manifestation of the new theories on " Direct Action." " The socialist syndicats have wrested the vote of the Chamber by the pressure of rebellion (*Coup d'émeutes*)" wrote the *Journal des Economistes*.[1] The revolutionary syndicalists themselves considered the agitation as an illustration of their methods, and the success obtained as a proof of the efficiency of the latter. The report to the Congress of Bourges (1904) read :

Under the pressure of the workingmen the Government, till then refractory to the reform, capitulated. . . . To-day it is an accomplished fact; wherever syndicalist action was exercised with perseverance and energy, the employment bureaus have gone. This fact is characteristic. The General Confederation has the merit, thanks to the immense effort of the interested themselves, of having obtained a reform in a relatively short time, if it is compared with the slowness with which everything concerning the workingmen is done.[2]

The policy of the General Confederation, however, had opponents within the Confederation itself. A struggle for supremacy between the two tendencies was inevitable, and it took place at the very next Congress of the Confederation at Bourges (1904).

The report presented to the Congress of Bourges showed that the Confederation had made considerable progress since 1902. It counted now 53 Federations of industries and trades, and National syndicats (against 30 in 1902), 15 isolated syndicats, and 110 *Bourses du Travail*, a total of 1,792 syndicats (against 1,043 in 1902),

[1] *Journal des Economistes* (November, 1903), p. 315.
[2] *XIV Congrès National Corporatif* (Bourges, 1904), p. 8.

with 150,000 members. The Section of Federations of industries had received in dues for the two years, 11,076 francs; its total budget amounted to 17,882 francs; the Section of *Bourses du Travail* had collected in dues 9,016 francs and . had a total budget of 12,213 francs. The *Voix du Peuple* was now self-supporting, and had increased the number of its subscriptions. The Congress of Bourges, for the first time, was organized on the financial resources of the syndicats without municipal or governmental subsidies.

It was known before that the Congress of Bourges would discuss the question of methods, and both sides, the revolutionary syndicalists and those who were called "reformists," made all efforts possible to obtain a majority at the Congress. There were 1,178 mandates from as many syndicats. This was the system of representation adopted by the Statutes of the Confederation in 1902. At its Congress the Confederation resolves itself into an association of syndicats; the Federations and Bourses disappear and their constituent elements, the syndicats, take their place. Each syndicat—no matter how large or how small—has one vote; and one delegate may represent as many as ten syndicats. At the Congress of Bourges the 1,178 mandates were distributed among 400 delegates, of whom 350 came from the Provinces and 50 from Paris.

The attack on the Confederal Committee was led by M. Keufer, the delegate and secretary of the Typographical Union (*La Fédération du Livre*). He accused the Confederal Committee of violating the statutes, of being partial and biased and of trying in every way to harm the *Fédération du Livre*, because the latter pursued "reformist" methods. "Yes," said M. Keufer, "we prefer the reformist method, because we believe that direct and violent action, commended by the anarchists, will cost thousands of workingmen their lives, without assuring durable results."[1]   He insisted that it was necessary to try conciliatory methods before declaring strikes and to solicit the help of representatives in the legislative bodies. He showed that, on the one hand, even the revolutionary syndicalists were compelled by circumstances to use such methods, while the *Fédération du Livre*, on the other hand, did not shrink from strikes and from direct action, when that was inevitable. M. Keufer was supported by M. Lauche, the delegate of the machinists, and by M. Guerard, the delegate of the railway workers.

The accusations of the "reformists" were repudiated by a number of revolutionary syndicalists who reaffirmed in their speeches adherence to the ideas, described in the preceding chapters, on the State, on direct action, etc. They were the victors, and the report of the Confederal Committee was approved by 812 votes against 361 and 11 blank.

The main struggle, however, centered on the question of proportional representation. This question had been brought up at previous Congresses by the delegates of some larger syndicats. At one time even some of the revolutionary syndicalists had advocated proportional representation as a means of finding out the real strength of the various tendencies in the Confederation. But after the Confederation became decidedly revolutionary, the revolutionary syndicalists became decidedly opposed to proportional representation which they now regarded as a move on the part of the "reformist" element to obtain control of the Confederation.[2]

[1] *XIV Congrès Corporatif* (Bourges, 1904), pp. 95–6.
[2] *Mouvement Socialiste* (Nov., 1904), p. 61.

Proportional representation was defended by the delegates of the Typographical Union, of the Machinists and of the Railway Workers. They criticised the statutes adopted at Montpellier which gave every organization, regardless of its numbers, one vote only in the Confederal Committee. This system, they declared, vitiated the character of the Confederation, and gave predominance to the minority. They claimed that the delegates in the Confederal Committee expressed the opinions shared by a small proportion only of the organized workingmen and that the Confederation was, therefore, a tool in the hands of a few " turbulent " individuals. They demanded that some system of proportional representation should be adopted which should give every organization a number of votes in the Confederal Committee proportional to the number of its members.

The opponents of proportional representation argued that this system would stifle the small syndicats; that all syndicats were of equal value from the point of view of the economic struggle, because small syndicats often achieve as much, and even more, than large ones; they pointed out that proportional representation would make necessary continual changes in the number of delegates in the Confederal Committee, because the effective force of the syndicats is in constant flux and that it would be impossible to find out the true figures. They claimed that proportional representation could not be applied to economic life, because it was no fault of any one trade or industry if only a few thousand workers were employed in it, while other industries required hundreds of thousands of workingmen. Even from the point of view of strength, they argued, a small syndicat may have more value than a large one because it may embrace a larger proportion of workingmen employed in the trade. The opponents of proportional representation repudiated the assertion that only the small syndicats were with them and pointed out that some of the largest federations, as the Metallurgical Federation with 11,500 members, the Federation of Marine with 12,000 members and others, were against proportional representation.

The opponents of proportional representation carried the day and the proposition of "reformist" delegates was rejected by a vote of 822 against 388 (one abstained).

The Congress of Bourges thus sanctioned the revolutionary character of the Confederation. The "reformists" frankly admitted that they had suffered a defeat and attributed it to the fact that two-thirds of the delegates were new men in the movement and under the influence of the anarchists.[1]   The revolutionary syndicalists triumphed, and extolled the historical significance of the Congress of Bourges which, in their opinion, was a "landmark" in the history of syndicalism.

The Congress of Bourges adopted a resolution which was to concentrate the attention of the Confederation for the next two years on one question: an eight-hour working day. The Committee appointed by the Congress to consider the question reported that two ways of obtaining an eight-hour day had been indicated. One proposed to prepare a bill to be presented to the public authorities and to organize public meetings in order to show the government that public opinion demanded the passage of the law. This method was rejected by the Committee because ever since 1889, workingmen had presented such petitions to the public authorities on the first of May, but without any results whatsoever.

On the contrary, the other "direct" method which

---

[1] A. Keufer, *Le Mouvement Socialiste* (Nov., 1904), p. 93.

recommended the workingmen to "hold aloof" from the public authorities, and to exert all possible pressure "on their adversaries" was adopted by the Committee. The Committee argued that the experience with the employment agencies had shown that this method gave better results. The report of the Committee read:

If the recent campaign has resulted in the suppression of the employment bureaus, it is because the movement was becoming dangerous.

Every day employment bureaus were abolished, anonymous violence was committed against the owners of the offices (*placeurs*), a considerable number of shops were damaged, numerous collisions took place between the police and the workingmen, Paris was in a state of siege, and it was in order to calm this agitation that Parliament voted a law making it permissive for the municipalities to abolish the employment bureaus.[1]

The Committee, therefore, recommended that the same method be used to obtain an eight-hour day, that big manifestations be organized all over France on the 1st of May, 1905, and that afterwards an active propaganda be carried on by a special commission appointed for that purpose by the Confederal Committee "in order that beginning with the 1st of May, 1906, no workingman should consent to work more than eight hours a day nor for a wage below the minimum established by the interested organizations."[2] The recommendation of the Committee was adopted by the Congress with an amendment of Pouget which still more emphasized the "direct" method to be used.

[1] *XIV Congrès Corporatif* (Bourges, 1904), pp. 205-6.
[2] *Ibid.*, p. 207.

To carry out the decisions of the Congress, the Confederal Committee appointed a special commission to direct the movement for an eight-hour day. The Commission sent out a questionnaire to all syndical organizations, asking all those who were in favor of the movement to lend their help. A number of manifestoes, posters and pamphlets were published and spread abroad in tens of thousands of copies in which the meaning of the movement and its importance were explained. In the trade-journals, in the cars, in the streets, and wherever possible, brief mottoes were posted, such as: "Eight hours of work means more rest and more health," "To work more than eight hours means to lower your wages," etc. On the *Bourse du Travail* of Paris a big placard was put up with the words: "From the first of May, 1906, we shall not work more than eight hours." Delegates were sent out on repeated tours into the province to carry on the propaganda and agitation. On the first of May, 1905, over 150 meetings were arranged in different parts of France at which the question of the eight-hour day was considered.

As May 1, 1906, neared, the agitation in the country became more and more intense. A number of events helped to increase the agitation. In March, 1906, a catastrophe occurred in the mining districts of Northern France which resulted in the loss of workingmen's lives. A strike accompanied by violence followed. In April, the letter carriers of Paris struck, causing some disorganization in the service for a few days.

Toward the end of April the number of strikes and manifestations increased in Paris. The agitation was exploited by the enemies of the government and particularly by the monarchist papers. The Government of M. Clemenceau, on the other hand, tried to discredit the movement by spreading rumors that a plot against the Republic had been discovered in which monarchists and leaders of the Confederation were involved. The *Voix du Peuple* published a protest of the Confederal Committee against this accusation. Nevertheless the government searched at the same time the houses of Monarchists, Bonapartists and of leading members of the Confederation, and on the eve of the first of May, it arrested Griffuelhes, Pouget, Merrheim and other syndicalists together with a number of well-known monarchists.

The first of May found Paris in a state of siege. Premier Clemenceau had collected numerous troops in the capital. Since the days of the Commune Paris had not seen so many. Among the bourgeoisie a real panic reigned. Many left Paris and crossed the Channel. Those who remained in Paris made provision for food for days to come. The papers spoke of the "coming revolution" which the General Confederation of Labor was to let loose on society.[1]

The strike movement was very wide. According to official statistics, the agitation of the Confederation affected 2,585 industrial establishments and involved 202,507 workingmen. The sweep of the movement may be grasped from the following table giving the statistics of strikes in France since 1892 :

[1] *Journal des Debats* (27 April, 1906), p. 769.

Year	Number of strikes	Number of establishments	Number of workingmen
1892	261	500	50,000
1893	634	4,286	170,123
1894	391	1,731	54,576
1895	405	1,298	45,801
1896	476	2,178	49,851
1897	356	2,568	68,875
1898	368	1,967	82,065
1899	740	4,290	176,826
1900	902	10,253	222,714
1901	523	6,970	111,414
1902	512	1,820	212,704
1903	567	3,246	123,151
1904	1,026	17,250	271,097
1905	830	5,302	177,666
1906	1,309	19,637	438,466
1907	1,275	8,365	197,961 [1]

The movement assumed various forms in different trades. The printers, for instance, pursued their conciliatory methods and obtained a nine-hour day in about 150 towns. In some trades the strikes developed a more or less acute character and continued for several months after the first of May.

Some of the "reformists" declared that the movement was a complete failure.[2]   According to official statistics,[3] the results of the strike movement were as follows:

Demand	Success			Compromise			Failure		
	Strikes	Establishments	Strikers	Strikes	Establishments	Strikers	Strikes	Establishments	Strikers
8 hour day..............	2	5	45	13	1,970	25,520	88	7,556	109,786
9 hour day..............	36	135	2723	28	994	30,750	45	755	17,023
10 hour day..............	40	582	7409	16	220	2,000	27	368	7,251
	78			57			160		

[1] Statistique des Grèves, 1893–1908.

[2] XV Congrès National Corporatif (Amiens, 1906), p. 103.

[3] Statistique des Grèves, 1906, pp. 774 et seq.

The revolutionary syndicalists did not claim much material success, but they argued that this had not been expected. The main purpose of the movement, they asserted, was, " by an immense effort, to spread among the large mass of workingmen the ideas which animate the militant groups and the syndical organizations. The problem to be solved, at first, was, thus, by means of a vigorous propaganda to reach the workingmen who had remained indifferent to the syndicalist movement."[1] And this task, in the opinion of the revolutionary syndicalists, had been accomplished. The agitation had aroused the workingmen in all parts of France.

In September, 1906, the Congress of the Confederation met at Amiens. The report of the secretary showed continued progress of the Confederation since 1904. The Section of Federations of industries now counted 61 federal organizations with 2,399 syndicats and 203,273 members. The dues collected by this section for the two years amounted to 17,650 francs; and its total budget to 20,586 francs. The section of the Federation of Bourses consisted now of 135 Bourses with 1,609 syndicats; it collected in dues 11,821 francs, and had a total budget of 15,566 francs.

The report of the Confederal Committee again called forth the attacks of " reformist " syndicalists, but was approved by 781 votes against 115 (21 blank and 10 contested). But the main question which absorbed the largest part of the work of the Congress was the relation of the General Confederation of Labor to the Socialist Party.

This question had again assumed a new character. The International Socialist Congress of Amsterdam (1904)

---

[1] *XV Congrès Corporatif* (Amiens, 1906), p. 3.

had exhorted and advised the French Socialists to accomplish as soon as possible the unification of their separate parties into one national Socialist Party.   In April,
1905, a "Congress of Unification" was held at Paris, at
which the *Parti Socialiste de France* and the *Parti Socialiste Français* formed the *Parti Socialiste Unifié.*   A
common program was accepted and a new form of organization elaborated.   At its first Congress in Chalons in
October, 1905, the Unified Party counted 35,000 paying
members distributed in 2,000 groups, 67 federations and
77 departments.   In the elections of 1906 the Unified
Party obtained an increase of votes and elected 54 members to Parliament.

It now seemed to many that there was no reason for
the General Confederation of Labor to keep aloof from
the Socialist Party.   The reason heretofore given was
that the divisions in the Socialist Party disorganized the
syndicats, but since the Socialist Party was now unified,
the reason lost all significance, and it seemed possible to
establish some form of union between the two organizations. The question was taken up soon after the unification of tbe Socialist Party by the "Federation of Textile
Workers" who had it inserted in the program of the
coming Congress of Amiens.   The question was discussed
for some time before the Congress in the socialist and
syndicalist press, and the decision that would be taken
could have been foreseen from the discussion.

M. Renard, the Secretary of the "Federation of Textile Workers," defended the proposition that permanent
relations should be established between the General Confederation and the Unified Socialist Party.   His argument was that in the struggle of the working-class for
emancipation, various methods must be used, and that
various forms of organization were accordingly neces-

sary. The syndicat, in his opinion, could not suffice for all purposes; it was an instrument in economic struggles against employers, but by the side of this economic action, political action must be carried on to obtain protective labor legislation. For this purpose he considered it necessary to maintain relations with the Socialist Party, which had "always proposed and voted laws having for their object the amelioration of the conditions of the working-class as well as their definitive emancipation."[1] Besides, argued M. Renard, "if a revolutionary situation should be created to-day," the syndicats now in existence, with their present organization could not "regulate production and organize exchange," and "would be compelled to make use of the machinery of the government." The co-operation of the Confederation with the Socialist Party, therefore, was useful and necessary from the point of view both of the present and of the future.

M. Renard repudiated the accusation that he meant to introduce politics into the syndicats or to fuse the latter in the Socialist Party. On the contrary, he accused the Confederal Committee of carrying on political agitation under the cover of neutrality. Against this "special politics" his proposition was directed. "When anti-militarism is carried on," said M. Renard, "when anti-patriotism is indulged in, when [electoral] abstention is preached, it is politics."[2] This anarchistic policy has prevailed since the "libertarians have invaded the Confederation and have transformed the latter into a war-engine against the Socialist Party. The Federation of Textile Workers wants to put an end to the present state of affairs."[3]

[1] *XV Congrès Corporatif* (Amiens, 1906), pp. 135-6.
[2] *Ibid.*, p. 134.   [3] *Ibid.*, p. 165.

The proposition of the Textile workers was combated by revolutionary and "reformist" syndicalists alike. M. Keufer, who had bitterly attacked the revolutionary syndicalists at Bourges (1904), now fought the political syndicalists. He agreed with M. Renard that political action was necessary though he did not place "too great hopes in legislative action and in the intervention of the State;" still he thought that the latter was inevitable, and alluded to the fact that the revolutionary syndicalists themselves were constantly soliciting the intervention of the public authorities. But to secure a successful parallel economic and political action, M. Keufer believed that it was better for the Confederation to remain entirely independent of the Socialist Party, and he proposed a resolution repudiating both "anarchist and anti-parliamentarian agitation" and permanent relations with any political party.[1]

The revolutionary syndicalists in their turn criticised the part assigned to the syndicat both by the political syndicalists and by the "reformists." They emphasized the "integral" and revolutionary rôle of the syndicat which makes it unnecessary and dangerous to conclude any alliance with any political party. They denied that the Confederal Committee was carrying on an anarchist propaganda. Said M. Griffuelhes:

Keufer insists very much on the presence of libertarians in the Confederal Committee; they are not so numerous as the legend has it; this is only a stratagem to arouse the fear of an anarchist peril which does not exist. On the contrary, the vitality of the Confederation is the result of a coöperation of various political elements. When, after the entrance of M.

[1] *XIV Congrès Corporatif* (Amiens, 1906), pp. 154–157.

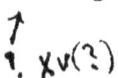

Millerand into the government, the latter began its policy of "domesticating" the workingmen, a coalition of Anarchists, Guesdists, Blanquists, Allemanists and other elements took place in order to isolate the government from the syndicats. This coalition has maintained itself and has been the very life of the Confederation.[1]

The proposition of the Textile Federation was rejected by 724 votes against 34 (37 blank). The defeat for the political syndicalists was complete. By an overwhelming majority of 830 against 8 (one blank), the Congress adopted the following proposition of Griffuelhes:

The Confederal Congress of Amiens confirms article 2 of the constitution of the General Federation.

The C. G. T. groups, independent of all political schools, all the workingmen who are conscious of the struggle to be carried on for the disappearance of the wage system. . . .

The Congress considers that this declaration is a recognition of the class struggle which, on an economic basis, places the workingmen in revolt against all forms of exploitation and oppression, material and moral, put into operation by the capitalist class against the working class.

The Congress makes this theoretic affirmation more precise by adding the following points:

With regard to the every-day demands, syndicalism pursues the coördination of the efforts of the workingmen, the increase of the workingmen's welfare through the realization of immediate ameliorations, such as the diminution of working hours, the increase of wages, etc.

But this is only one aspect of its work; syndicalism is preparing the integral emancipation which can be realized only by the expropriation of the capitalist class; it commends as a means to this end the general strike, and considers that the

[1] *XV Congrès Corporatif* (Amiens, 1906), p. 167.

syndicat, now a group of resistance, will be in the future the group of production and of distribution, the basis of social organization.

The Congress declares that this double task of every-day life and of the future follows from the very situation of the wage-earners, which exerts its pressure upon the working-class and which makes it a duty for all workingmen, whatever their opinions or their political and philosophical tendencies, to belong to the essential group which is the syndicat; consequently, so far as individuals are concerned, the Congress declares entire liberty for every syndicalist to participate, outside of the trade organization, in any forms of struggle which correspond to his philosophical or political ideas, confining itself only to asking of him, in return, not to introduce into the syndicat the opinions which he professes outside of it.

In so far as organizations are concerned, the Congress decides that, in order that syndicalism may attain its maximum effectiveness, economic action should be exercised directly against the class of employers, and the Confederal organizations must not, as syndical groups, pay any attention to parties and sects which, outside and by their side, may pursue in full liberty the transformation of society.

The vote on this resolution showed that all parties interpreted the resolution in their own way. To the "reformists" it meant complete political neutrality, to the political syndicalist it emphasized the liberty of political action outside the syndicat; the revolutionary syndicats saw in the resolution the "Charter of French Syndicalism" in which their theories were succinctly formulated.

After the Congress of Amiens the General Confederation continued its policy of direct action. During 1907 it helped the movement for a law on a weekly rest (*Repos Hebdamodaire*) which was carried on by the commercial employees and by workingmen of certain trades. The movement expressed itself often in street demonstrations and riotous gatherings and brought the Confederation into conflict with the government.

The government of M. Clemenceau took a determined attitude towards the Confederation. Papers like the *Temps* called upon the government to dissolve the Confederation. "Against syndicalism," wrote the *Temps*, "are valid all the arguments of law and of fact as against anarchy." Members of the Confederal Committee were arrested here and there for incendiary speeches and for anti-militaristic propaganda. In the Chamber of Deputies the Confederation was the subject of a heated debate which lasted several days, and in which radicals, conservatives, socialists, and members of the government took part.

The Confederal Committee in its turn vehemently attacked the government. In June, 1907, troubles occurred among the wine-growers in the south of France, and blood was shed. The Confederal Committee launched a manifesto against the government with the heading, "Government of Assassins," in which it praised one of the regiments that had refused to shoot into the crowd at the order of the officers.

The government instituted legal proceedings against twelve members of the Confederal Committee for "insults to the army." The trial took place in February, 1908; all the accused were acquitted.

In June, 1908, a strike in one of the towns near Paris, Draveuil, occasioned the intervention of the police. Shooting took place, one workingman was killed, one mortally wounded, and several others severely wounded. On the 4th of June the Confederal Committee published a protest calling the government "a government of assassins" and Premier Clemenceau, "Clemenceau the murderer" (*Clemenceau le Tueur*) and called upon the syndicats to protest against the action of the government. As the strike in Draveuil was among workingmen of the building trades, the "Federation of the Building Trades," the most revolutionary syndical organization in France, took the lead in the movement, seconded by the Confederal Committee. Manifestations took place at the funerals of the killed workingmen in Draveuil and Villeneuve St. George (neighboring communes) in which bloody collisions with the police were avoided with difficulty. The "Federation of the Building Trades" and many members of the Confederal Committee advocated a general strike as a protest against the action of the government.

Meanwhile the strike at Draveuil was going on. On the 27th of July a collision between the police and the strikers again took place, and the "Federation of Building Trades" decided upon a general strike and upon a demonstration for the 30th of July. Some members of the Confederal Committee, the Secretary Griffuelhes, for instance, were opposed to the manifestation, but the decision was taken against their advice.

The manifestation of Villeneuve St. George resulted in a violent collision; there were many killed and wounded. The agitation grew, and the Confederal Committee together with the federal committee of the Building Trades called upon the other trades to join them in a general strike to be continued as a protest against the "massacres." The call of the Confederal Committee was only partly followed.

The events of Villeneuve St. George aroused the press and the government against the Confederation. The "Confederal Committee," wrote the *Temps*, "is not an instrument for trade conquests. It is a purely insurrectional Committee. It should be treated as such." The government arrested all the leading members of the Confederal Committee.

On the 4th of August, as a move against the government, the Confederal Committee which constituted itself after the arrests and of which M. Luquet was temporary secretary, admitted the Federation of Miners with 60,000 members into the Confederation. The Federation of Miners had for some time expressed its wish to enter the Confederation, but certain difficulties, more or less personal, had stood in the way. After Villeneuve St. George these difficulties were smoothed and the adherence of the Miners to the Confederation was made possible.

The events of Villeneuve St. George aroused some protests within the Confederation. The collisions and the bloodshed were ascribed by the opponents of the Confederal Committee to revolutionary methods and "anarchist" tactics. The polemics between the "reformist" and "revolutionary" elements which had not ceased since the Congress of Amiens now became more and more bitter.

In September, 1908, the Congress of the Confederation met at Marseilles. The reports to the Congress showed that the Section of Federations of industries counted 68 federal organizations with 2,586 syndicats and 294,398 members; total receipts amounted to 24,-719 francs. The Section of Bourses counted 157 *Bourses du Travail* with 2,028 syndicats and with a budget of 16,081 francs.

The Congress of Marseilles expressed its sympathy with the arrested members of the Confederation, and "denounced before the entire public the abominable procedures" of the government, The reports of the Confederal Committee were approved by 947 with none against and 109 blanks, "not because the members of the Confederal Bureau were arrested, but because the acts of the Bureau and of the Confederal Committee were the expression of the mandate entrusted to them."

The Congress of Marseilles rejected the proposition to apply the principle of proportional representation which was again advanced. It discussed the question of industrial and trade unionism and decided in favor of the former, inviting all trade federations to fuse into industrial federations.

But the main question which agitated the Congress was that of anti-militarism. At Amiens (1906) an anti-militaristic resolution introduced by Yvetot (Secretary of the Section of *Bourses du Travail*) had been passed. But it was passed in a hurry, as there was no time to discuss it, and it raised strong opposition among the "reformist" elements. It was taken to the Congress of Marseilles, therefore, for another discussion.

The Congress of Marseilles accepted the resolution introduced by Yvetot. The resolution read:

The Congress of Marseilles, repeats and renders more precise the decision of Amiens, namely:

Considering that the army tends more and more to take the place of the workingmen on strike in the factory, in the fields, in the workshop, when it has not the function of shooting them, as in Narbonnes, Raon-L'Etape, and Villeneuve St. George;

Considering that the exercise of the right to strike will be only a fraud as long as the soldiers agree to substitute the workers in civil work and to massacre the workingmen; the Congress, keeping within purely economic limits, recommends the instruction of the recruits (*jeunes*) in order that on the day when they put on the military uniform they should be convinced that they should remain nevertheless members of the family of workingmen and that in the conflict between capital and labor their duty is not to use their arms against their brethren, the workingmen;

Considering that the geographical boundaries are modifiable at the will of the possessors, the workingmen recognize only the economic boundaries separating the two class-enemies —the working class and the capitalist class.

The Congress repeats the formula of the International: " The workingmen have no fatherland;" and adds:

That whereas, consequently, every war is but an outrage (*attentat*) against the workingmen; that it is a bloody and terrible means of diverting them from their demands, the Congress declares it necessary, from the international point of view, to enlighten the workingmen, in order that in case of war they may reply to the declaration of war by a declaration of a revolutionary general strike.[1]

The resolution was adopted by 681 votes against 421 and 43 blank.   Many voted against the resolution because of its anti-patriotic character, though they accepted the part bearing upon the use of the army in strikes.

In November, 1909, the government freed the arrested members of the Confederal Committee, but they did not regain their former positions of authority.   In February, 1909, the " reformist " elements succeeded in electing as secretary of the Confederation their candidate, M. Niel, who was once a revolutionary but had become more moderate.   M. Niel was elected by a majority of one vote, and his position was very difficult in the Confederal Committee.   He aimed, as he expressed it, to bring about " moral unity" in the Confederation, but was hampered in his activities by the revolutionaries and not sufficiently supported by the " reformists."

In March, 1909, the Post Office employees went on

[1] *XVI Congrès National Corporatif*, p. 213.

strike. The Confederation took no part in the movement but invited the workingmen to sympathize with the strikers. The strike was successful, and the government promised to consider the grievances of the Post Offiℓe employees whose main demand was the removal of the Secretary of the Department.

The promises of the government were unofficial, and the strikers after some time claimed that the government had not kept its word. A second strike followed in May, but there was less enthusiasm among the employees, and a failure was inevitable. The leaders of the strike appealed to the Confederation for help. The Confederal Committee invited the workingmen of Paris to go out on a general strike, but the invitation of the Confederation found very little response, and the Post Office employees returned to work.

The failure was ascribed to the "reformists", M. Guérard,[1] secretary of the Railway Workers, and to M. Niel, who had delivered a speech on the eve of the general strike declaring that the miners were not ready for it. This speech, the revolutionaries alleged, produced an impression disastrous for the general strike. The bitter criticism of the revolutionists forced Niel to resign on May 28, 1909. The election of Jouhaux secured the triumph of the revolutionary syndicalists once more.

The dissensions between "reformists" and revolutionaries" became still more acute after the resignation of M. Niel. The rumor that the "reformist" syndicats would leave the Confederation circulated more persistently than before, The "reformists" formed in July, 1909, a *Comité d' Union Syndicaliste* to react against the anarchistic syndicalism, to realize the union of workingmen,

---

[1] M. Guérard, once revolutionary, had become moderate.

independent of all politics, in the exclusively economic and industrial domain.[1] The situation was considered very critical by both friends and enemies of the Confederation.

The struggle of tendencies and personalities within the Confederation came to a climax at the next congress held at Toulouse from Oct. 3 to Oct. 10, 1910. The greater part of the time of the congress was consumed in discussing the resignation of Niel, the accusations against the former secretary Griffuelhes, and the quarrels of "reformists" and revolutionists generally. Both sides were disgusted with the proceedings, but hoped that the atmosphere of mutual hostility and distrust would be cleared thereby, and that a new period of harmonious action would be the result.

The Congress was hardly over, when a strike unexpectedly broke out among the railway men of the *Paris-Nord*. The National Syndicat of Railway workers had been considering the advisability of a general strike for some time, but was postponing action in the hope of effecting a peaceful settlement. The Syndicat of railway workers was among the so-called "reformist" syndicats, and its leaders laid great stress on peaceful negotiations with employers and on soliciting the coöperation of the government. The demands of the railway men were: an increase in wages, one day of rest in the week, the retroactive application of the old-age pension law passed in 1909, and several other concessions relating to conditions of work and matters of discipline. The railway companies had refused to meet the representatives of the railway men, and M. Briand, who was Premier at the time, advised the officials of the railway union that he

[1] G. Weill, *Histoire du Mouvement Social du France*, 386.

could do nothing to make the railway companies change their attitude. The leaders of the syndicat, however, were still continuing their efforts to bring pressure to bear upon the companies, when their plans were frustrated by the sudden outbreak on the railroad system known as Paris-Nord.

The strike, begun in Paris on October 10, rapidly spread over the system Paris-Nord. The next day the strike committee ordered a general railroad strike, and the order was followed on October 12 by the Western system of railroads. On October 13 M. Briand arrested the members of the strike committee and ordered the striking railway men under colors, thus putting them under martial law. A second strike committee automatically took the place of the leaders who were arrested, but it did not display much energy. Besides, the response to the strike order on the eastern and southern railroad lines was very slight, and towards the end of the week the strike was practically defeated. By order of the second strike committee work was resumed on all lines on October 18.

The failure of the railway strike was a heavy blow not only to the syndicat of Railway Workers, but to the general labor movement of France. It resulted in the disorganization of one of the strongest syndicats and added fuel to the dying embers of factional strife. The revolutionary elements in the Confederation attributed the failure of the strike to the hesitating tactics of the " reformist " leaders and to the intervention of the socialist politicians who tried to make political capital out of the strike situation. The " reformists," on the other hand, accused the revolutionists of precipitating the strike and of defeating the general movement by hasty action on the Paris-Nord. Two facts, however, stand out clear: first, that the Confederation of Labor did not direct the strike, which was a purely trade movement largely dominated by reformist and political elements; secondly, that the strike was defeated mainly by the quick and energetic action of M. Briand, who treated the strike as a revolt, sent soldiers to replace the strikers, and mobilized the latter for military service.

The dissensions provoked by the railway strike accentuated the "crisis" in the General Confederation of Labor and hampered its activities. Still, amid these internal struggles, the Confederal Committee made persistent efforts to carry out the program of action which was outlined for it at the congress of Toulouse. During 1910–1911 it carried on a relentless campaign against the old-age pension law which was passed in April, 1910. The French workingmen were opposed to the age limit imposed by the law (65 years), to the system of capitalization, and to the obligatory deductions of the worker's contribution from his wages. The campaign was effective to the extent of forcing several important modifications in the law in favor of the workers.

At the same time the Confederation carried on a campaign against the high cost of living ascribing it to speculation and to the protective system. Meetings were held throughout France, and demonstrations were arranged; in many places bread riots took place in which the leaders of the Bourses and of the Confederal Committee took part.

But the greatest part of the energy of the Confederation was directed against the wave of militarism and nationalism which began to sweep France after the incident of Agadir in the summer of 1910. The Confederation of Labor felt that the labor movement in general and the revolutionary tendencies in particular were en-

dangered by the nationalist spirit and military excitement which was stirring the country. Meetings were
organized all over France to protest against war and
militarism; several international meetings were arranged
in Berlin, Madrid, Paris, and London, at which speakers
representing all European countries spoke against war
and in favor of international peace. The idea of a general strike in case of war was revived and agitated in the
syndicalist organizations as a warning to the French
government.   *However(?)*

In September, 1912, the twelfth congress of the Confederation was held at Toulouse. The report of the
Confederal Committee showed that the Confederation
was not making as much progress as before. The
growth of the General Confederation of Labor in relation to the general labor movement of the country may
be judged from the following table :

Year	Total Number of Syndicats in France	Total Number of Organized Workingmen in France	Number of Federations of industry adhering to Confederation	Syndicats adhering to Confederation	Members of Confederation
1902....	3,680	614,204	30	1,043	
1904....	4,227	715,576	53	1,792	150,000
1906....	4,857	836,134	61	2,399	203,273
1908....	5,524	957,102	63	2,586	294,398
1910....	5,260	977,350	57	3,012	357,814
1912....	5,217	1,064,000	53	2,837	400,000

The slackening in the growth of the Confederation

was attributed partly to the persistent persecutions of the government, but in the main to internal dissensions and struggles. As a result of the latter, many of the old militants who had taken a leading part in the syndicalist organizations had become disillusioned and had left the movement. Many of the syndicats had lost in membership, and new syndicats were formed with great difficulty.

The supreme effort of the Congress of Toulouse was, therefore, to assert once more the leading ideas of syndicalism and to unite all labor elements upon a common platform of action. A long debate between representatives of the various tendencies took place in consequence of which the Congress reaffirmed the resolution of Amiens (1906) known as the " charter of syndicalism." [1] The most important resolution, however, was that in favor of a general movement for the reduction of hours of labor, particularly for the establishment of the " English week " (La semaine Anglaise, i. e. half holiday on Saturday). The Confederal Committee was authorized to carry on a campaign similar in character to the Campaign of 1906 in favor of the eight hour day. To meet the necessary expenses the dues were raised to ten francs per thousand members for each Federation of industry and to seven francs per thousand members for each Departmental Union.

The discussion at the Congress of Toulouse showed very clearly that the leaders of the syndicalist organizations were becoming tired of perennial debates and that they were anxious to save the Confederation from its present critical condition by a vigorous campaign for shorter hours, which would appeal to the mass of working men and women. The Confederal Committee, how-

[1] See page 183.

ever, has not been very successful in this since the congress of Toulouse, for two principal reasons: the militaristic excitement of Europe and the general industrial depression. During 1913, the Confederation was engaged in fighting the increase in military expenses and particularly the passage of the the three years' military service law. In May and June a number of revolts took place in the barracks, mainly among the soldiers who would have been released in 1913, had not the new law been made retroactive. The government accused the Confederation of instigating the revolts of the soldiers, and made numerous arrests among the leaders of the principal syndicats in Paris and in the province. The Confederation repudiated complicity in the revolts, but asserted its right to maintain relations with the soldiers by means of the *Sou du Soldat*. A number of protest meetings were held in Paris and other cities against the new military law, and there can be little doubt that this agitation resulted in the modifications of the law which practically reduced the actual time of service by several months.

At the same time, the activities of the General Confederation of Labor during 1913 revealed a conscious determination to steer clear of hazardous movements of a revolutionary character. In July, 1913, the Federations of industries and the Bourses du Travail held their third annual Conference in Paris, at which questions of administration and policy were discussed. A number of delegates demanded that a general strike be declared on September 24, when the soldiers ought to have been released from the barracks. This proposition was defeated as an unwise measure. Among those who spoke against the proposition were some of the ablest representatives of the revolutionary syndicalists, like Jouhaux, the general secretary; Merrheim, the secretary of the Federation of the metal industry, and others. The cautious action of the Confederation incensed the anarchist groups who had supported the Confederation all along, and they began to criticise the latter for "turning to the right." The leaders of the Confederation, however, explained their action not by any change in ideas, but by a desire to hew to the line of strictly labor demands for the time being.

While making efforts to increase its strength at home, the Confederation of Labor has been endeavoring in recent years to spread the ideas of French syndicalism abroad, and has been watching with great interest the new tendencies in the labor movement of England and the activities of the Industrial Workers of the World in the United States. Its main efforts outside of France, have been exerted at the conferences of the International Secretariat of Labor. These conferences have been held every two years since 1903 by the secretaries of the adhering National Trade Union Centers.[1] The General Confederation took part in the Conference of Dublin in 1903, but sent no delegates to the Conferences of Amsterdam (1905) or of Christiana (1907) because these conferences refused to discuss the questions of the general strike and of anti-militarism. The relations of the Confederation to the International Secretariat have been much discussed at the Congresses of the Confederation and in the press. The Congress of Marseilles, though approving the policy of the Confederal Committee, recommended that the latter enter into closer relations with the International Secretariat. Since then

[1] The first two conferences were held at Balberstadt (1900) and at Stuttgart (1902).

the Confederation has taken part in the Conferences of Paris in 1909,[1] Budapest (1911), and Zurich (1913).

In the International organization the Confederation tries to enforce its views on the general strike and advocates the organization of International Labor Congresses. Its ideas meet here, however, with the opposition of American, English, German and Austrian trades unions. The latter are the more numerous. Germany pays dues to the International Secretariat for 2,017,000 organized workingmen; the United States for 1,700,000; England for 725,000; Austria for 480,000; France for 340,000. The total number of organized workingmen affiliated with the International Secretariat is 6,033,500.[2]

[1] An account of the Paris conference is given in Mr. Gompers' *Labor in Europe and America* (New York, 1910).

[2] These figures are for 1911.

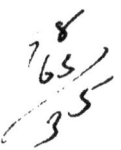

CHAPTER VIII

CHARACTER AND CONDITIONS OF REVOLUTIONARY SYNDICALISM

THE history of the General Confederation of Labor as told in the preceding chapters has brought out in a general way the character of revolutionary syndicalism and the conditions which have influenced its rise and development. It remains now in this last chapter to emphasize the principal points and to strengthen them by a more complete analysis of facts and conditions.

It has been maintained throughout this work that revolutionary syndicalism was created by a *bloc* of revolutionary elements in the Confederation. This character of a *bloc* has been denied by many. Those hostile to the Confederation are anxious to create the impression that the latter is exclusively the creation and the tool of the anarchists. Others more or less impartial fail to acknowledge the part played in the movement by the non-anarchist elements. Some anarchists themselves are only too glad to be considered the creators of the movement and to maintain a view which is a tribute to their organizing ability and to their influence.

Many revolutionary syndicalists, however, protest against being considered anarchists. Some of them are active members of the Unified Socialist Party. Others do not belong to the Socialist party, but have never been connected with the Anarchists. They are revolutionary syndicalists, "pure and simple." And these two other elements are by no means less influential in the Confederation than the Anarchists.

The three elements enumerated have somewhat different ways of regarding revolutionary syndicalism. To the anarchists revolutionary syndicalism is but a partial application of anarchist ideas. M. Yvetot, secretary of the section of Bourses, said at the recent Congress of Toulouse (1910) : " I am reproached with confusing syndicalism and anarchism. It is not my fault if anarchism and syndicalism have the same ends in view. The former pursues the integral emancipation of the individual ; the latter the integral emancipation of the workingman. I find the whole of syndicalism in anarchism. " [1]

To the revolutionary socialists in the Confederation, syndicalism is the primary and fundamental form of revolutionary socialism. It does not exclude, however, other forms ; on the contrary, it must be completed by the political organization of the Socialist party, because it has no answer of its own to many social problems,

The third group of revolutionary sydicalists regards revolutionary syndicalism as self-sufficing and independent of both anarchism and socialism. This group, like the first, emphasizes the fact that there is an irreconcilable antagonism between syndicalism and political socialism. " It is necessary, " writes Jouhaux, secretary of the Confederation, " that the proletariat should know that between parliamentary socialism, which is tending more and more toward a simple democratization of existing social forms, and syndicalism, which pursues the aim of a complete social transformation, there is not only divergence of methods, but particularly divergence of aims. [2]

Those who consciously call themselves revolutionary syndicalists belong to one of the groups described, and

[1] *La Vie Ouvrière*, 20 Oct., 1910, p. 483 ; *XVII Congrès National Corporatif* (Toulouse, 1910), p. 226.

[2] L. Jouhaux, *Le Terrassier*, 20 June, 1911.

the three groups constitute the *bloc* spoken of above. To understand revolutionary syndicalism means to understand this *bloc* of revolutionary elements, how it was made possible, why it is maintained, and what conditions have secured for it the leadership in the General Confederation of Labor.

It has been shown in the preceding chapters that since 1830 a considerable part of the French workingmen, the so-called "militant" workingmen, have always cherished the hope of a "complete" or "integral" emancipation which should free them from the wage-system and from the economic domination of the employer. The desire of independence had guided the life of the journeyman under the guild-system, and its birth under modern economic conditions is natural enough to need no explanation. But while under the guild-system this desire had an individualistic character, under the technical conditions of the present time it necessarily led to collectivist ideas. With the development of highly expensive means of production, only an insignificant number of workingmen could hope to become economically independent by individual action, and the only way to attain economic freedom and equality for all pointed to the collective appropriation of the means of production and to the collective management of industrial activities.

The insistence on economic freedom—in the sense indicated—runs through all the literature of the French Labor Movement. It is not only and not so much the inequality of wealth, the contrasts of distribution that stimulate the militant workingmen to their collectivist hopes, as it is the protest against the "arbitrariness" of the employer and the ideal of a "free workshop." To attain the latter is the main thing and forms the program of the General Confederation as formulated in the first clause of its statutes.

The sensitiveness to economic inferiority is increased in the French militant workingmen by the fact that in a country like France economic distinctions are combined with social distinctions. Owing to the traditions of the past, economic classes are separated by a number of other elements, in which intellectual, social and other influences combine and which transform the economic classes into social classes. The aspiration towards economic equality increases, therefore, in volume and becomes a striving after social equality.

The historical traditions of France combined with the impatience for emancipation explain the revolutionary spirit of the French socialist workingman. All who have come into contact with French life have convinced themselves of the power which the revolutionary traditions of the past exert over the people. The French workingman is brought up in the admiration of the men of the Great Revolution; his modern history is full of revolutionary secret societies, of insurrections, and of revolutionary struggles. He cherishes the memory of the Revolution of 1848, his indignation is aroused by the story of the Days of June, his pity and sympathy are stimulated by the events of the Commune. Looking backward into the history of the past century and a half, he can only get the feeling of political instability, and the conviction is strengthened in him that "his" revolution will come just as the revolution of the "Third-Estate" had come. Combined with the desire to attain the "integral" emancipation as soon as possible, these conditions engender in him the revolutionary spirit.[1]

[1] On the peculiar character of French history see Adams, *Growth of the French Nation;* Berry, *France since Waterloo;* Barrett Wendell, *France of To-day.*

The revolutionary spirit predisposes the socialist workingman to a skeptical attitude toward parliamentary
action which rests on conciliation and on compromise
and is slow in operation. He seeks for other methods
which seem to promise quicker results. The methods
themselves may change; they were insurrection once,
they are now the general strike. But the end they serve
remains the same: to keep up the hope of a speedy
liberation.

The distrust of parliamentary methods has been
strengthened in the French socialist workingman by
another fact. The French workingmen have seen their
political leaders rise to the very top, become Ministers
and Premiers (*e. g.*, Millerand, Vivani, Briand), and then
turn against their " comrades " of old. The feeling has
been thereby created in the socialist workingmen that
parliamentary methods are merely a means to a brilliant
career for individuals who know how to make use of
them.

The mistrust of " politicians " finds some nourishment
in the fact that the political leaders of the Socialist.
movement are generally the " intellectuals," between
whom and the workingmen there is also some antagonism. The " intellectuals " are thrown out upon the social
arena principally by the lower and middle bourgeoisie
and generally enter the liberal professions. But whether
lawyer, writer, doctor or teacher, the French " intellectual " sooner or later enters the field of " politics " which
allures him by the vaster possibilities it seems to offer.
In fact, the " intellectual " has always been a conspicuous
figure in the history of French Socialism. As a socialist
poet, Pierre Dupont, sang,

> " Socialism has two wings,
> The student and the workingman. "

And as the socialist ideas have spread, the number of "intellectuals" in the socialist movement has been constantly increasing.

The "two wings" of the Socialists, however, cannot perfectly adapt themselves to one another. The "intellectual" generally lacks the "impatience for deliverance" which characterizes the socialist workingman. The "intellectual" is bound by more solid ties to the *status quo;* his intellectual preoccupations predispose him to a calmer view of things, to regard society as a slow evolutionary process. Besides, the "intellectual" takes pride in the fact that he supplies "the proletariat with fresh elements of enlightenment and progress"; he is inclined, therefore, to dominate the workingman as his "minor brother", and to advocate methods which secure his own predominant part in the movement. Parliamentary action is the field best adapted to his character and powers. The socialist workingman, on the other hand, protests against the tendencies of the "intellectual", particularly against the dominating impulses of the latter. He is anxious to limit the powers of his leaders, if possible, and to create such forms of organization as shall assure his own independence.

When the syndicats began to develop in France, the revolutionary workingmen seized upon them as a form of organization particularly adapted to their demands. The syndicat was an organization which could take up the ideal of social emancipation; in the general strike, which the syndicat seemed to carry within itself, there was a method of speedy liberation; the syndicat excluded the "intellectuals" and above all by its "direct action" it maintained and strengthened the revolutionary spirit and safeguarded the revolutionary ideal from the compromises and dangers to which politics and the parliamentary socialists subjected it.

These conditions: the hope of social emancipation, the impatience for deliverance, the revolutionary spirit, and the defiance of the "intellectuals" and of the "poli-. ticians," gave and continue to give life to revolutionary syndicalism. They brought into being the "revolutionary *bloc*" in the General Confederation of Labor and maintain it there. Of course, differences of temperament and shadings of opinion exist. On the one extreme are those who are most vehement in their propaganda and who combat the Socialist party; on the other, are the revolutionary socialists who are disposed to cooperate with the parliamentary socialists, but who want to have an independent organization to fall back upon in case of disagreement with the political party. But differing in details, the revolutionary elements agree in the main points and they stamp upon the Confederation the character which it bears and which is described in the terms "revolutionary syndicalism."

The opponents of the revolutionary syndicalists claim that the latter are followed only by a minority in the General Confederation and that they maintain their leadership by means of the existing system of representation and by other more or less arbitrary devices. This statement, however, cannot be proved in any satisfactory way.

The best way of obtaining the exact number of revolutionary syndicalists in the Confederation would seem to be by means of an analysis of the votes taken at the Congresses. This method, however, is defective for several reasons. In the first place, not all the syndicats adhering to the Confederation are represented at the Congresses. At the Congress of Bourges (1904), 1,178 syndicats out of 1,792 were represented; at the Congress of Amiens, 1,040 out of 2,399; at the Congress of Marseilles, 1,102 out of 2,586, and at the Congress of Toulouse, 1,390 out of 3,012. It is evident, therefore, that even if all the votes were taken unanimously, they would still express the opinion of less than half the syndicats of the Confederation.

In the second place, the votes of the Confederation being taken by syndicats, to get the exact figures it would be necessary to know how many syndicats in each federation are revolutionary or not, and what is the proportional strength of both tendencies in each syndicat. This is impossible in the present state of statistical information furnished by the Confederation.

At the Congress of Amiens, for instance, the vote approving the report of the Confederal Committee (Section of Federation) stood 815 against 106 (18 blanks). This vote is important, because to approve or to reject the report meant to approve or to reject the ideas by which the General Confederation is guided.

Now, an analysis of the vote at Amiens shows that while some organizations voted solidly for the Confederal Committee, none voted solidly against it and that the votes of many organizations were divided. But even the number of those represented by the unanimous vote of their syndicats cannot in the most cases be ascertained. For instance, the agricultural syndicats cast their 28 votes for the Confederal Committee; the report of the Confederal Committee gives the Federation of Agricultural Laborers 4,405 members; but the same report says that the Federation consisted of 106 syndicats; of these 106 syndicats only 28 were represented at the Congress, and how many members they represented there is no possibility of ascertaining. The same is true of those Federations in which the syndicats did not cast the same vote.

This difficulty is felt by those who try to prove by figures that the Confederation is dominated by a minority. M. Ch. Franck, for instance, calculates that at the Congress of Marseilles 46 organizations with 716 mandates representing 143,191 members obtained the majority for the *statu quo* against the proposition of proportional representation ; while the minority consisted of 15 organizations with 379 mandates representing 145,440 members. In favor of the anti-militaristic resolution, he calculates further, 33 organizations with 670 mandates representing 114,491 members obtained the majority against 19 organizations with 406 mandates representing 126,540 members. But he is compelled to add immediately : " These figures have no absolute value, because we have taken each organization in its entirety, while in the same federation some syndicats have not voted with the majority"; he thinks that the proportion remains nevertheless the same because he did not take into consideration the divisions on each side.[1]

The last assumption, however, is arbitrary, because the syndicats dissenting on the one side may have been more numerous than those not voting with the majority on the other side; the whole calculation, besides, is fallacious, because it takes the figures of the federations in their entirety, while only a part of the syndicats composing them took part in the votes.

The attempt, therefore, to estimate the exact number of the revolutionary syndicalists in the Confederation must be given up for the present. The approximate estimate on either side can be given. According to M. Pawlowski,[2] 250,000 members of the Confederation (out

[1] *Op. cit.*, pp. 345-6.
[2] A. Pawlowski, *La Confédération Générale du Travail* (Paris, 1910), p. 51.

of 400,000) repudiate the revolutionary doctrine; the revolutionary syndicalists, on the other hand, claim a majority of two-thirds for themselves. The impartial student must leave the question open.

It must be pointed out, however, that the system of representation which exists now in the Confederation affects both revolutionary and reformist syndicalists in a. more or less equal degree. At the Congress of Amiens, for instance, the *Fédération du Livre*, with its 10,000 members, had 135 votes; the Railway Syndicat, with its 24,275 members, had only 36 votes; these two organizations were among the "reformists" who combated the Confederal Committee. On the other hand, the revolutionary Federation of Metallurgy had 84 votes for its 14,000 members, but the Federation of Marine, which is also revolutionary, disposed of six votes only for its 12,-000 members. The revolutionary syndicalists, therefore, may be right in their assertion that proportional representation would not change the leadership of the Confederation. This belief is strengthened in them by the fact that in all so-called "reformist" organizations, as the *Fédération du Livre*, the Railway Syndicat, etc., there are strong and numerous revolutionary minorities. It is often asserted that only the small syndicats, mostly belonging to the small trades, follow the revolutionary syndicalists. This assertion, however, is inexact. An examination of the syndicats which are considered revolutionary shows that some of them are very large and that others belong to the most centralized industries of France. For instance, the Federation of Building Trades is the most revolutionary organization in the Confederation; at the same time it is the most numerous, and its members pay the highest dues (after the

Fédération du Livre) in France.[1]   The revolutionary
Federation of Metallurgy is also one of the large organizations in the Confederation and belongs to an industry
which is one of the most centralized in France. The
total horse-power of machines used in the metallurgic
industries has increased from 175,070 in 1891 to 419,128
in 1906; the number of establishments has diminished
from 4,642 in 1891 to 4,544 in 1906; that is, the total
horse-power of machinery used in every industrial establishment has increased during this period from 38 to
92;[2] the number of workingmen per industrial establishment has also increased from 508 in 1896 to 697 in 1901
and to 711 in 1906. In fact the metallurgic industry
occupies the second place after the mining industry
which is the most centralized in France.[3]

A diversity of conditions prevails in the industries to
which the other revolutionary organizations belong.
On the other hand, the so-called reformist organizations,
the Federation of Mines, the *Fédération du Livre*, the
Federation of Employees, differ in many respects and are
determined in their policy by many considerations and
conditions which are peculiar to each one of them.

The influence of the revolutionary syndicalists, therefore, can be explained not by special technical conditions,
but by general conditions which are economic, political
and psychological. To bring out the relation of these
conditions to the syndicalist doctrine it is necessary to
analyze the latter into its constituent elements and to
discuss them one by one.

The fundamental condition which determines the policy

[1] *Mouvement Socialiste*, May, 1911.

[2] E. Thery, *Les Progrès Économiques de la France* (Paris, 1909), p.
181.

[3] *Journal des Economistes*, Jan., 1911, p. 133.

of " direct action " is the poverty of French syndicalism. Except the *Fédération du Livre*, only a very few federations pay a more or less regular strike benefit; the rest have barely means enough to provide for their administrative and organizing expenses and can not collect any strike funds worth mentioning. In 1908, for instance, there were 1,073 strikes; of these 837 were conducted by organized workingmen. Only in 46 strikes was regular assistance assured for the strikers, and in 36 cases only was the assistance given in money.[1] The French workingmen, therefore, are forced to fall back on other means during strikes. Quick action, intimidation, *sabotage*, are then suggested to them by their very situation and by their desire to win.

The lack of financial strength explains also the enthusiasm and the sentiments of general solidarity which characterize French strikes. An atmosphere of enthusiasm must be created in order to keep up the fighting spirit in the strikers. To the particular struggle in any one trade a wider and more general significance must be attributed; it must be interpreted as a partial manifestation of a more general class-struggle. In this way the determination to struggle on is strengthened in those who strike and a moral justification is created for an appeal to the solidarity of all workingmen. These appeals are made constantly during strikes. Subscription lists are kept in the *Bourses du Travail*, in the Confederal Committee on Strikes, and are opened in the workingmen's and socialist newspapers whenever any big strike occurs.

New means to make up for the lack of financial resources are constantly devised. Of these means two which

---

[1] *Statistique des Grèves*, 1909, vi–vii.

have come into existence within recent years are the *soupes communistes* and the "exodus of children." The *soupes communistes* are organized by the *Bourses du Travail* and consist of meals distributed to those on strike. The *soupes communistes* permit the feeding of a comparatively large number of strikers at small expense. Distribution occurs at certain points. The workingmen, if they wish, may take their meals home. The last Conferences of the section of Bourses have discussed the question how to organize these *soupes communistes* more systematically and as cheaply as possible.

The "exodus of children" consists in sending away the children of the strikers to workingmen of other towns while the strike is going on. It has been used during several strikes and attracted widespread attention. The "exodus of children" relieves the strikers at home and and creates sympathy for them over the country at large.

Financial weakness has also led French syndicats in recent yeas to reconsider the question of co-operation. Various federations have expressed themselves at their federal congresses in favor of "syndicalist co-operatives" in which all associates are at the same time members of the syndicat and organized on a communist basis. The main argument brought forward in favor of such co-operatives is the support they could furnish to workingmen on strike.

The poverty of the French syndicats is the result of the reluctance of the French workingmen to pay high dues. In the *Fédération du Livre*, which has the highest dues, every member pays a little over two francs a month. In other federations the dues are lower, coming down in some organizations to 10 centimes a month. In recent years there has been a general tendency in all federations to increase dues, but the efforts of the syndicalist functionaries in this direction have met with but slow and partial success.

The reluctance to high dues is in part the result of the comparatively low wages which prevail in France. Another factor is the psychology of the French workingman. "Our impulsive and rebellious (*frondeur*) temperament," wrote the Commission which organized the Congress of Montpellier, "does not lend itself to high dues, and if we are always ready to painful sacrifices of another nature, we have not yet been able to understand the enormous advantages which would follow from strong syndicalist treasuries maintained by higher assessments."[1] The French workingmen are conscious of their peculiar traits, and the literature of the syndicalist movement is full of both jeremiads and panegyrics with regard to these traits, according to the speaker and to the circumstances. The French workingmen recognize that they lack method, persistence and foresight, while they are sensitive, impulsive and combative.[2]

The result of this psychology is not only poor syndicats, but syndicats weak in other respects. Many syndicats are but loosely held together, are easily dissolved and are composed of a more or less variable and shifting membership. The instability is increased of course by the absence of benevolent features in the syndicats. The *Fédération du Livre* alone pays sick and other benefits.

The weakness of the syndicats predisposes the French workingmen to more and more generalized forms of struggle. Syndicats on strike impelled by the desire to increase their forces try to involve as many trades and workingmen as possible and to enhance their own

---

[1] *XIII Congrès National Corporatif*, 1902, pp. 30-31.

[2] *X Congrès National Corporatif*, p. 203; *XII Congrès National Corporatif*, pp. 15, 29, 44.

chances by enlarging the field of struggle. This is why such general movements, as the movement for an eight-hour day in 1906, described in the preceding chapter, are advocated by the syndicats. The latter feel that in order to gain any important demand they must be backed by as large a number of workingmen as possible. But in view of their weakness, the syndicats can start a large movement only by stirring up the country, by formulating some general demand which appeals to all workingmen. The same conditions explain in part the favor which the idea of the general strike has found in the syndicats.

Such forms of struggle must necessarily bring the syndicats into conflict with the State, particularly in France where the State is highly centralized and assumes so many functions. With a people so impulsive as the French, the intervention of the forces of the State in the economic struggles must inevitably lead to collisions of a more or less serious character. The result is a feeling of bitterness in the workingmen towards the army, the police and the government in general. The ground is thus prepared for anti-militaristic, anti-State and anti-patriotic ideas.

The organized workingmen are a minority of the working-class. Still they must act as if they were the majority or the entirety of the workingmen. The contradiction must be smoothed over by some explanation, and the theory of the "conscious minority" arises to meet the situation. The weaker the syndicats and the more often they are exposed to the danger of dissolution the greater the necessity of the theory. A disorganized syndicat generally leaves behind a handful of militant workingmen determined to keep up the organization. The theory of the "conscious minority" is both a stimulus to and a justification for the activities of these persistent " militants."

To the conditions described the French love of theory, of high-sounding phrases, and of idealistic formulas must be added. For a Frenchman it is not sufficient to act under necessity: the act must be generalized into a principle, the principles sytematized, and the system of theory compressed into concise and catching formulas. And once abstracted, systematized and formulated, the ideas become a distinct force exerting an influence in the same direction as the conditions to which they correspond.

When all this is taken into account, it is easier to understand the influence of the revolutionary syndicalists. It is insufficient to explain their leadership by clever machinations of the Confederal Committee, as M. Mermeix and many others do. It is quite true that the Confederal Committee tries to maintain its power by all means possible. It sends out delegates to Federal Congresses, on conference tours over the country, to assist workingmen on strikes, etc. In most cases it sends only men who represent the revolutionary ideas of the Committee and who, therefore, strengthen the influence of the latter by word and deed. It is also true that in most *Bourses du Travail* the secretaries are revolutionary and that they help to consolidate the influence of the Confederal Committee. But these secretaries have not usurped their power. They are elected because they have come to the front as speakers, writers, organizers, strike-leaders, etc. And they could come to the front only because conditions were such as to make their ideas and services helpful.

Whatever one's attitude to the Confederation, one must acknowledge the results it has achieved. The strike statistics of France, given in the following table, show the following facts:

Period	Per cent of strikes which failed	Per cent of strikers who lost their strikes
1890–1899	44.61	38.63
1891–1900	43.86	34.17
1892–1901	42.69	35.42
1893–1902	42.48	31.75
1894–1903	42.13	26.98
1895–1904	40.24	25.09
1896–1905	39.07	23.76
1897–1906	38.05	25.91
1898–1907	38.14	25.37
1899–1908	35.79	25.83

Of course, these results can not be attributed entirely to the action of the Confederation. On the other hand, the influence of the Confederation on the improvement of general conditions of employment, on social legislation, etc., is undeniable. "In all branches of human activity," says M. Pawlowski, "wages have risen with a disconcerting and disquieting rapidity."[1] The agitation for the eight-hour day and the rising of 1906 hastened the vote on the weekly rest, induced the government to consider the application of the ten-hour day, popularized the practice of the "English week," etc.[2]

Whether the same or better results could have been obtained by "reformist" methods, is not a question to be considered, because in most cases the syndicats have no choice. A strike once begun, the character of the struggle is determined by conditions which exist and not by any that would be desirable. This is proved by the fact that very often the so-called "reformist" syndi-

---

[1] A. Pawlowski, *La Confédération Générale du Travail*, p. 130.
[2] *Ibid.*, p. 123.

cats carry on their struggles in the same way and by the same methods as do the revolutionary ones.

The comparative influence of the Confederation explains the fact why the " reformists " do not leave the organization, though they are bitter in their opposition to the revolutionists. The "reformists " feel that they would thereby lose a support which is of value to them. Besides, in many cases such an act would lead to divisions within the reformist federations, all of which, as already indicated, contain considerable revolutionary minorities.

The revolutionary syndicalists, however, are in their turn compelled to make concessions to those exigences of the labor movement which have nothing to do with revolutionary ends. Of course, the revolutionary syndicalists are workingmen and they are interested in the immediate improvement of economic conditions. But there can be little doubt that the leaders and the more conscious and pronounced revolutionary syndicalists are mainly interested in their revolutionary ideal, in the abolition of capitalism and of the wage-system. The struggles for higher wages, shorter hours, etc., are a necessity which they must make a virtue of while awaiting the hoped-for final struggle. And when they theorize about the continuity of the struggles of to-day with the great struggles of to-morrow, when they interpret their every-day activities as part of a continuous social warfare, they are merely creating a theory which in its turn justifies their practice and preserves their revolutionary fire from extinction.

But theorizing does not essentially change the character of all syndicalist activities. The Confederal Committee must attend to the administrative and other questions, such as the questions of *viaticum*, of the label, etc. The necessities of the syndical movement often lead the members of the Confederal Committee into the antechambers of Parliament or into the private rooms of the Ministers whose assistance is solicited. The most revolutionary federations can not help entering into negotiations with employers for the settlement of strikes. In practice, therefore, the distinction between "revolutionary" and "reformist" syndicalists is often obscured, because both act as they must and not as they would.[1]

This must not be interpreted to mean that there is any conscious hypocrisy or undue personal interest on the part of the leaders of the revolutionary syndicalists. On the contrary, the most bitter opponents of the Confederation must admit that the reverse is true. "However one may judge their propaganda," says M. Mermeix, "he is obliged to acknowledge the disinterestedness of the libertarians who lead the syndicalist movement. They do not work for money. . . ."[2] There is also no field in the Confederation for political ambition. Still the movement has its demands which require suppleness and pliability on the part of the leaders and which make impossible the rigid application of principles.

On the other hand, the revolutionary syndicalists have in the syndicats a tremendous force for their revolutionary ends. The close relation of syndical life to all political and economic problems gives the Confederal Committee the opportunity to participate in all questions of interest. The high cost of living, the danger of a war, the legislative policy of the government, troubles among the wine-growers, any public question, indeed, is the occasion for the intervention of the Confederal Com-

---

[1] This is admitted by both sides. See reports of last Congress held at Toulouse (1910), p. 111.

[2] Terrail-Mermeix, *La Syndicalisme contre le Socialisme* (Paris, 1907), p. 231.

mittee. The latter appears, then, also as a revolutionary organization which is always ready to criticise, to discredit and to attack the government, and which is openly pursuing the overthrow of existing institutions in France. And when one keeps in mind the indefatigable anti-militaristic and anti-patriotic propaganda carried on by the *Bourses du Travail* all over the country, the revolutionary character of the Confederation may be fully appreciated.

What is the future that may be predicted for the General Confederation of Labor? Will the synthesis of revolutionism and of unionism that has been achieved in it continue more or less stable until the "final" triumph of the revolutionary syndicalists? Or will the latter be overpowered by the "reformist" elements who will impress their ideas on the Confederation and who will change the character of French syndicalism?

These questions cannot at present be answered. The movement is so young that no clear tendencies either way can be discerned. The two possibilities, however, may be considered in connection with the conditions that would be required to transform them into realities.

Those who predict a change in the character of French syndicalism generally have the history of English Trades Unionism in mind. They compare revolutionary syndicalism to the revolutionary period of English Trades Unionism and think of the change that came about in the latter in the third quarter of the past century. But the comparison is of little value, because the conditions of France are different from those of England, and because the international economic situation to-day is very different from what it was fifty years ago.

It is probable that if the French syndicats should develop into large and strong unions, highly centralized and provided with large treasuries, other ideas and methods would prevail in the syndicalist movement. But this change is dependent on a change in the economic life of France. France must cease to be "the banker of Europe," must cease to let other countries use its piled-up millions[1] for the development of their natural resources and industry, and must devote itself to the intensification of its own industrial activities. Such a change could bring about greater productivity, higher wages, and a higher concentration of the workingmen of the country. This change in conditions of life might result in a modification of the psychology of the French workingmen, though how rapid and how thorough-going such a process could be is a matter of conjecture. But whether France will or can follow the example of England or of Germany, in view of its natural resources and of the situation of the international market, it does not seem possible to say.[2] Besides, to change completely the character of French syndicalism, it would be necessary to wipe out the political history of France and its revolutionary traditions.

On the other hand, the triumph of the revolutionary syndicalists presupposes a total readjustment of groups and of interests. The Confederation counts now about 600,000 members. Official statistics count over 1,000,-000 organized workingmen in France. But it must be remembered that the federations underestimate their numbers for the Confederation in order to pay less, while they exaggerate their numbers for the *Annuaire Statistique* in order to appear more formidable. The Confederation, besides, for various reasons rejects a number of organizations which desire to join it. It may

[1] It is estimated that France has about 40,000,000,000 francs invested in foreign countries.

[2] See Preface to Second Edition.

be safe to say, therefore, that the Confederation brings under its influence the greater part of the organized workingmen of France.

But the total number of workingmen in .France, according to the Census of 1906, is about 10,000,000, of which about 5,000,000 are employed in industry and in transportation. The numbers of independent producers in industry, commerce, and agriculture is about 9,000,-000, of which about 2,000,000 are *petits patrons*. Over a million and a half persons are engaged in the liberal professions and in the public services.[1]

Among the latter the revolutionary syndicalists have met with success in recent years. The ideas of revolutionary syndicalism have gained adherents among the employees of the Post Office, Telegraph and Telephone, and among the teachers of the public schools. The recent Congresses of the teachers have declared themselves ready to collaborate with the workingmen for the realization of their ideal society. The following motion adopted by the recent Congress of Nantes, at which 500 delegates were present, is very characteristic: "The professional associations of teachers (men and women), employees of the State, of the Departments and of the Communes," reads the motion, "assembled in the *Bourses du Travail*, declare their sympathy for the working-class, declare that the best form of professional action is the syndical form; express their will to work together with the workingmen's organizations for the realization of the Social Republic."[2]

Also among the industrial and commercial middle classes there are some who look with favor on syndical-

---

[1] The active population in 1906 was over 20,000,000, out of a total population of over 39,000,000. *Journal des Économistes*, Jan., 1911.

[2] *L'Humanité*, August 8, 1911.

ism.   The French middle classes have for the last quarter
of a century tried to organize themselves for resistance
against the "financial feudalism" from which they suffer.
Several organizations have been formed among the small
merchants and masters, and in 1908 the "Association
for the Defense of the Middle Classes" was constituted.
The president of this Association, M. Colrat, wrote:
"The ideas of the bourgeois syndicalism on the future
are the same as those of the workingmen's syndicalism.
. . . Far from contradicting one another, the syndicalism of the middle classes and the syndicalism of the
working-classes reinforce each other in many respects,
and notwithstanding many vexations, they lead to a
state of relative equilibrium by a certain equality of opposing forces."[1] In the struggle against the big capitalists the leaders of the middle classes appear to be
ready to form an alliance with the working-class. There
can be little doubt, however, that the middle classes in
general are opposed to the revolutionary ideals of the
syndicalists.   To succeed, the revolutionary syndicalists
must bring about a change in the attitude of these
classes, for the history of France has shown that the
fear of "Communism" may throw the middle classes
into the arms of a Caesar.

Whatever possibility may become a reality, France seems
destined to go through a series of more or less serious
struggles.   Hampered by the elements which hark back
to the past and which have not yet lost all importance,
disorganized by the revolutionists who look forward to
the future for the realization of their ideal, the Republic
of France is still lacking the stability which could save
her from upheavals and from historical surprises.   The

[1] M. Colrat, *Vers l'équilibre social*, quoted by Mr. J. L. Puecht. "Le
Mouvement des Classes Moyennes," in *La Grande Revue*, Dec., 1910.

highly centralized form of government and the dominating position which Paris still holds in the life of France make such surprises easier and more tempting than would otherwise be the case. The process of social readjustment which is going on all over the world at present, therefore, must lead in France to a more or less catastrophic collision of the discordant elements which her political and economic history have brought into existence.

The struggle has already begun. The government of the Republic is determined to put an end to the revolutionary activities of the syndicalists. It is urged on by all those who believe that only the weakness of the Government has been the cause of the strength of the Syndicalists. On the other hand, the Syndicalists are determined to fight their battle to the end. What the outcome may be is hidden in the mystery of the future. *Qui vivra—verra.*

BIBLIOGRAPHY

* *Action Directe.* Revue Révolutionnaire Syndicaliste. Paris, July, 1903-August, 1904.

Annuaire Statistique. Ministère du Travail et de la Prévoyance Sociale. Paris.

Antonelli, E. *La démocratie sociale devant les idées présentes.* Paris, 1911.

Associations professionnelles ouvrières; office du Travail. Paris, 1899-1904.

Barberet, J. *Monographies professionnelles.* 4 vols. Paris, 1886.

Bataille Syndicaliste. Daily.

Berth, Edouard. *Les nouveaux aspects du socialisme.* Paris, 1908.

Blum, Leon. *Les congrès ouvriers et socialistes français.* Paris, 1901.

Bouglé, E. *Syndicalisme et démocratie.* Paris, 1908.

Bourdeau, J. *Entre deux servitudes.* Paris, 1910.

Bourgin, H. *Le socialisme et la concentration industrielle.* Paris, 1911.

* Boyle, James. *Minimum Wage and Syndicalism.* Cincinnati, 1913.

Bracq, J. Ch. *France under the Republic.* New York, 1910.

Brants, Victor. *La petite industrie contemporaine.* Paris, 1902.

Breton, J. L. *L'Unité Socialiste.* Vol. 7 of Histoire des partis socialistes, ed. by Zévaès. Paris, 1912.

Brooks, John Graham. *American Syndicalism.* New York, 1913.

Buisson, Etienne. *La grève générale.* Paris, 1905.

Chaboseau, A. *De Babeuf à la Commune.* Volume 1 of Histoire des partis socialistes, edited by Zévaès.

* Challaye, Félicien. *Syndicalisme révolutionnaire et syndicalisme réformiste.* Paris, 1909.

Chambre des Députés, Débats Parlementaires.

Charnay, Maurice. *Les Allemanistes.* Vol. 5 of Histoire des partis socialistes, edited by Zévaès.

Clay, Sir Arthur. *Syndicalism and Labor.* London, 1912.

Cole, G. D. H. *The World of Labor.* London, 1913.

Commission Ouvrière de 1867, recueil des procès-verbaux. 2 vols. Paris, 1868-69.

Congrès national des syndicats ouvriers tenu à Lyon en Octobre, 1886, compte rendu Lyon, 1887.

Congrès général des organisations socialistes, compte rendu. Paris, 1899.

Congrès (deuxième) général des organisations socialistes françaises tenu à Paris de 28 au 30 Septembre, 1900, compte rendu. Paris, 1901.

Congrès (troisième) général des organisations socialistes françaises tenu à Lyon du 26 au 28 mar., 1901, compte rendu. Paris, 1901.

Congrès national des syndicats tenu à Marseilles du 19 au 22 Octobre, 1892, compte rendu. Paris, 1909.

Congrès national du Parti Ouvrier tenu à Paris du 11 au 14 Juillet, 1897, compte rendu.

Congrès national corporatif (IVe de la Confédération Générale du Travail), tenu à Rennes, compte rendu. Rennes, 1898.

Congrès national corporatif (Ve de la Confédération), tenu à Paris, compte rendu. Paris, 1900.

Congrès national corporatif (VIe de la Confédération), tenu à Lyon, compte rendu. Lyon, 1901.

Congrès national corporatif (VIIe de la Confédération), tenu à Montpellier, compte rendu. Montpellier, 1902.

Congrès national corporatif (VIIIe de la Confédération), tenu à Bourges, compte rendu. Bourges, 1904.

Congrès national corporatif (IXe de la Confédération), tenu à Amiens, compte rendu. Amiens, 1906.

Congrès national corporatif (Xe de la Confédération), tenu à Marseille, compte rendu. Marseille, 1909.

Congrès national corporatif (XIe de la Confédération), tenu à Toulouse, compte rendu. Paris, 1911.

Congrès national corporatif (XIIe de la Confédération), tenu à Havre, compte rendu. Paris, 1913.

Congrès socialiste international tenu à Paris du 23 au 27 septembre, 1900. Paris, 1901.

Connay, J. *Le Compagnonnage, son histoire, ses mystères.* Paris, 1909.

Cornélissen, Ch. "Ueber den internationalen Syndikalismus." *Archiv für Sozialwissenschaft und Sozialpolitik.* Tübingen, 1910.

Crouzel, A. *Etude historique, économique et juridique sur les coalitions et les grèves.* Paris, 1887.

Da Costa, Charles. *Les Blanquistes.* Vol. 6 of Histoire des partis socialistes, edited by Zévaès. Paris, 1912.

Delesalle, J. *Les Bourses du Travail et la C. G. T.* Paris.

Delessale, P. *L'action syndicaliste et les anarchistes.* Paris, 1900.

Déville, G. *Principes socialistes.* Paris, 1896.

Dijol, M. *Situation économique de la France, sous le régime protectioniste de 1892.* Paris, 1911.

Diligent, Victor. *Les orientations syndicales.* Paris, 1910.

Dru, Gaston. *La Révolution qui vient.* Paris.

Dubois, F. *The Anarchist Peril.* Tr. by Ralph Derechef. London.

Dubreilh, L. *La Commune.* Paris, 1908.

* Du-Cellier, M. *Histoire des classes laborieuses en France.* Paris, 1860.

Dufour. *Le Syndicalisme et la Prochaine Révolution.* Paris, 1913.

Économiste Français. Monthly.

Égalité. Periodical published from 1877 to 1881. Paris.

* Ely, R. T. *French and German Socialism.* New York, 1898.

Estey, James Arthur. *Revolutionary Syndicalism.* London, 1913.

* Faguet, E. *Le socialisme en 1907.* Paris, 1907.

Festy, Octave. *Le mouvement ouvrier au debut de la Monarchie de Juillet.* Paris.

Forces productives de la France. Conférences organisées a la Société des anciens élèves de l'Ecole libre des Sciences politiques. Paris, 1909.

Franck, Charles. *Les Bourses du travail et la Confédération Générale du Travail.* Paris, 1910.

Fribourg, E. E. *L'Association internationale des travailleurs.* Paris, 1871.

Garin, J. *L'anarchie et les anarchistes.* Paris, 1885.

Georgi, E. *Theorie und Praxis des Generalstreiks in der modernen Arbeiterbewegung.* Jena, 1908.

Grande Revue. Monthly.

Griffuelhes, V. *Voyage révolutionnaire; impressions d'un propagandiste.* Paris, 1910.

* Griffuelhes, V. *L'action syndicaliste.* Paris, 1908.

Griffuelhes, V. et Niel, L. *Les objectifs de nos luttes de classes.* Paris, 1909.

Guerre Sociale, La, revolutionary weekly edited by Gustave Hervé.

Guesde, J. *Le Socialisme au jour le jour.* Paris, 1899.

Guesde, J. et Lafargue, P. *Le programme du parti ouvrier.* Paris, 1897. 4th edition.

> Guillaume, James. *L'Internationale, documents et souvenirs.* 4 vols. Paris, 1905-10.

Hamon, A. *Le Socialisme et le congrès de Londres.* Paris, 1897.

Hanoteaux, G. *Modern France.* 4 vols. New York, 1903-09.

* Harley, J. H. *Syndicalism.* London, 1912.

Hervé, Gustave. *My Country, Right or Wrong.* English translation by Guy Bowman. London, 1911.

Hubert-Valleroux, P. *La Co-opération en France.* Paris, 1904.

* Humbert, Sylvain. *Le Mouvement Syndical.* Vol. 9 of Histoire des partis socialistes, edited by Zévaès. Paris, 1912.

Humbert, Sylvain. *Les Possibilistes.* Vol. 4 of Histoire des partis socialistes, edited by Zévaès. Paris, 1911.

L'Humanité. Socialist daily published since 1905. Contains many articles by revolutionary and reformist syndicalists.

Isambert, G. *Les idées socialistes en France de 1815 à 1848.* Paris, 1905.

Jouhaux, L. *Le Syndicalisme français.* Bruxelles, 1911.

Journal des Débats. Weekly.

Journal des Économistes. Monthly.

Kirkup, Th. *A History of Socialism.* Third edition. New York, 1906.

Kritsky. *L'Evolution du syndicalisme en France.* Paris, 1908.

Labusquière. *La Troisième République.* Paris, 1909.

Lagardelle, H. *L'Évolution des syndicats ouvriers en France.* Paris, 1901.

Lagardelle, H. *La grève générale et le socialisme.* Paris, 1905.

Lagardelle, H. *Le socialisme ouvrier.* Paris, 1911.

Lagardelle, H. "Die Syndikalistische Bewegung in Frankreich." *Archiv für Sozialwissenschaft und Sozialpolitik.* Tübingen, 1908.

Laurin, M. T. *Les Instituteurs et le syndicalisme.* Paris, 1908.

Lavy, A. *L'Oeuvre de Millerand.* Paris, 1902.

Leroy, Maxime. *Syndicats et Services Publics.* Paris, 1909.

Levasseur, E. *Histoire des classes ouvrières et d'industrie en France avant 1789.* 2 vols. Second edition. Paris, 1900.

Levasseur, E. *Histoire des classes ouvrières et d'industrie en France de 1789 à 1870.* 2 vols. Second edition. Paris, 1903.

Levine, Louis. "The Development of Syndicalism in America." *Political Science Quarterly,* September, 1913.

Levine, Louis. "Direct Action." *Forum.* New York, May, 1912.

Levine, Louis. "Syndicalism." *North American Review.* July, 1912.

Levine, Louis. "The Standpoint of Syndicalism." *Annals of the American Academy of Political and Social Science.* 1912.

Lewis, Arthur D. *Syndicalism and the General Strike.* London, 1912.

Libertaire, Le. Anarchist weekly.

Lorulot, André. *Le Syndicalisme et la transformation sociale.* Arcueil, 1909.

Louis, Paul, *Histoire du socialisme français.* Paris, 1901.

Louis, P. *Histoire du mouvement syndical en France.* Paris, 1907.

Louis, P. *Le syndicalisme contre l'état.* Paris, 1910.

Louis, P. "Die Einheitsbestrebungen im französischen Sozialismus." *Archiv für Sozialwissenschaft und Sozialpolitik.* Tübingen, 1909.

Macdonald, J. Ramsay. *Syndicalism.* 1912.

Méline, J. *The Return to the Land.* Tr. from the French. New York, 1907.

Milhaud, A. *La lutte des classes à travers l'histoire et la politique.* Paris.

Millerand, A. *Le socialisme réformiste français.* Paris, 1903.

Molinari, G. *Les Bourses du Travail.* Paris, 1893.

Molinari, G. *Le mouvement socialiste et les réunions publiques.* Paris, 1872.

Mouvement Socialiste. Published since 1899. Particularly valuable for students of revolutionary syndicalism.

Orry, Albert. *Les Socialistes Indépendant.* Vol. 8 of Histoire des partis socialistes, edited by Zévaès. Paris, 1911.

Parti Socialiste. Proceedings of annual conventions (1904-1913).

Pataud, E. et Pouget, E. *Comment nous ferons la révolution.* Paris, 1909. Translated into English by Charlotte and Frederick Charles, under title: *Syndicalism and the Co-operative Commonwealth.* London, 1913.

Pawlowski, A. *La confédération générale du travail.* Paris, 1910.

Pelloutier, F. *Le congrès général du parti socialiste français.* Paris, 1900.

Pelloutier, F. *Histoire des bourses du travail.* Paris, 1902.

Pelloutier, Maurice. *Fernand Pelloutier, sa vie, son oeuvre.* Paris, 1911.

Pelloutier, F. et M. *La vie ouvrière.* Paris, 1900.

Perdiguier, Agricol. *Le livre du compagnonnage.* Second edition. Paris, 1841.

Pierrot. *Syndicalism et révolution.* Second edition. Paris, 1908.

Pouget, E. *Le sabotage.* Paris, 1910. English translation by Arturo M. Giovannitti.

Pouget, E. *Les bases du syndicalisme.* Paris.

Pouget, S. *Le syndicat.* Paris.

Pouget, E. *Le parti du travail.* Paris.

Pouget, E. *La confédération générale du travail.* Paris, 1908.

Prolo, Jacques. *Les Anarchistes.* Vol. 10 of Histoire des partis socialistes, edited by Zévaès. Paris, 1912.

Proudhon, J. P. *De la capacité politique des classes ouvrières.* Paris, 1865.

Renard, Georges. *La république de 1848.* Paris, 1907.

Renard, G. *Syndicats, trades unions, et corporations.* Paris, 1909.

Rénault, Ch. *Histoire des grèves.* Paris, 1887.

Revue Socialiste. Monthly.

Revue Syndicaliste. Monthly published from May, 1905, to January, 1910.

Séances du Congrès Ouvrier de France. Session de 1876. Paris, 1877.

Seilhac, Leon de. *Syndicats ouvriers, fédérations, bourses du travail.* Paris, 1902.

Seilhac, Leon de. *Les congrès ouvriers en France.* Paris, 1899.
Seilhac, Leon de. *Le monde socialiste.* Paris, 1896.
Severac, G. *Guide pratique des syndicats professionnels.* Paris, 1908.
Smith, L. *Les coalitions et les grèves.* Paris, 1885.
Socialiste, Le. Organe central du Parti Socialiste Français.
Sombart, Werner. *Socialism and the Social Movement.* English tr. by M. Epstein. New York, 1909.
Sorel, G. *L'avenir socialiste des syndicats.* Revised edition. Paris, 1901.
Sorel, G. *La décomposition du marxisme.* Paris, 1908.
Sorel, G. *Illusions du progrès.* Paris, 1911. Second edition.
Sorel, G. *Réflexions sur la violence.* Paris, 1910. Second edition.
Sorel, G. *Introduction à l'économie moderne.* Second edition. Paris.
Sorel, G. *La révolution dreyfusienne.* Second edition. Paris, 1911.
Sorel, G. "La polémique pour l'interprétation du marxisme." *Revue internationale de sociologie.* Paris, 1900.
Sorel, G. "L'éthique du socialisme." *Morale Sociale.* Paris, 1900.
Spargo, John. *Syndicalism, Industrial Unionism, and Socialism.* New York, 1913.
Stoddart, J. T. *The New Socialism.* London, 1910.
St. Leon, E. Martin. *Le compagnnonnage.* Paris, 1901.
Syndicalisme et socialisme. Paris, 1908.
Syndicat et syndicalisme; opinions par Griffuelhes, Yvetot, Pouget, etc. Paris.
Terrail-Mermeix. *La France socialiste.* Paris, 1886.
Terrail-Mermeix. *Le syndicalisme contre le socialisme.* Paris, 1907.
Terrassier, Le. Published bi-weekly by some syndicats of the building-trades.
Temps Nouveaux. Anarchist weekly.
Thomas, Albert. *Le second empire.* Paris, 1907.
Tridon, André. *The New Unionism.* New York, 1913.
Vie Ouvrière. Revue Syndicaliste Bi-mensuelle. Paris.
Villetard, Edmond. *History of the International.* Tr. from the French, 1874.
Voix du Peuple. Organe de la Confédération Générale du Travail.
Warbasse, James Peter. *The Ethics of Sabotage.* Pamphlet. New York, 1913.
Ware, Fabian. *The Worker and his Country.* London, 1912.
Warin, Robert. *Les Syndicats Jaunes.* Paris, 1908.
Webb, Sydney and Beatrice. *An Examination of Syndicalism.* London, 1912.
Webb, B. and S. *History of Trade Unionism.*
Weill, George. *Histoire du mouvement social en France.* First edition, 1904. Second edition, 1910.

Weill, G. "Die Formen der Arbeiterbewegung in Frankreich." *Archiv für Sozialwissenschaft und Sozialpolitik.* Tübingen, 1909.

Yvetot, George. *A. B. C. syndicaliste.* Paris.

Yvetot, G. *Manuel du soldat.* Paris.

Zévaès, Alexandre. *Histoire des partis socialistes en France.* 11 volumes. Paris, 1911.

Zévaès, Alexandre. *Le Socialisme en France depuis 1871.* Paris, 1908.

Zévaès, Alexandre. *Le Syndicalisme Contemporain.* Paris, 1911.

Zévaès, Alexandre. *Le Socialisme en 1912.* Vol. 11 of Histoire des partis socialistes. Paris, 1912.

Zévaès, Alexandre. *De la semaine sanglante au Congrès de Marseille* (1871-1879). Vol. 2 of Histoire des partis socialistes, edited by Zévaès. Paris, 1911.

Zévaès, Alexandre. *Les Guesdistes.* Vol. 3 of Histoire des partis socialistes. Paris, 1911.

CPSIA information can be obtained
at www.ICGtesting.com
Printed in the USA
BVOW11s2050071117
499787BV00010B/78/P